CONSIDER CHICKEN KIEV

a gourmet's delight—but so calorific! A whopping 517 calories per serving (approximately) when prepared by the usual method.

RECONSIDER CHICKEN KIEV

a gourmet's delight—but only about 285 calories per serving prepared by Michele Evans' slimming recipe in the

AMERICAN CUISINE MINCEUR COOKBOOK

Chicken Kiev is just one of the delectable recipes you'll find in this innovative collection for those as concerned with their figures as their palates. These recipes are only the beginning. Michele Evans adapts all your favorites to this new, healthful cooking method. So begin to change your way of dining into a way of life with the AMERICAN CUISINE MINCEUR COOKBOOK.

Books by Michele Evans

American Cuisine Minceur Cookbook
The Slow Crock Cookbook

Published by
WARNER BOOKS

American Cuisine Minceur Cookbook

Michele Evans

WARNER BOOKS

A Warner Communications Company

WARNER BOOKS EDITION

Copyright © 1977 by Michele Evans
All rights reserved

ISBN 0-446-89456-7

Cover design by H. Youner

Cover photograph by J. West

Warner Books, Inc., 75 Rockefeller Plaza, New York, N.Y. 10019

Ⓦ A Warner Communications Company

Printed in the United States of America

Not associated with Warner Press, Inc. of Anderson, Indiana

First Printing: July, 1977

10 9 8 7 6 5 4 3 2 1

For John

Contents

Introduction

Without knowing it, I have been cooking *cuisine minceur* on and off for years. I simply called it sensible cooking. While testing recipes for the other cookbooks I've written, I have always gained a few pounds. As soon as I've finished with the testing, I've managed to shed the extra weight by preparing my food with less butter, cream, eggs, fats, starches, and sugar. What I've been doing, I've since discovered, is cooking the way that has revolutionized French cooking in the past few years: *cuisine minceur*. When I realized that the process had a name, I decided to put my own experiences on paper as an American adaptation of the new cuisine, using simple methods and mostly inexpensive ingredients.

While writing and testing recipes for this book, I actually lost five pounds. Though I was eating more than the average person does on the usual three-meals-a-day routine, I still lost weight. I also, not incidentally, created a truly revolutionary béarnaise sauce.

In recent years, Americans, who have become increasingly diet conscious, have been urged to try a succession of regimes all guaranteed to deliver effective weight loss. The diets range from the drinking man's diet through a university diet based almost exclusively on rice dishes, a bananas-only diet, the many variations on all-protein, etc., on down to fasting. Unfortunately, the above-mentioned diets are ones that can be adhered to for two weeks at the most and are certainly disagreeable. If there is a miracle to *cuisine minceur*, it is this: not only is it the way we should eat all the time for health and happiness, but it is surprisingly delicious.

What is
Cuisine Minceur?

Cuisine minceur (slimming cooking) is the modern common-sense approach to good cooking with minimum use of butter, eggs, cream, fats, starches, and sugar. These ingredients are used with the utmost discrimination, and the result is excellent dishes that are healthier, more easily digested, and less fattening. This revolutionary new approach originated with the talented young chef, Michel Guérard, who led the revolt against the excesses of classic French cooking. His theory was that dieting and *haute cuisine* need not be a contradiction in terms. By skillfully experimenting with the traditional recipes and methods of *la grande cuisine*, this master chef has kept the standards high but simplified the methods and minimized the use of rich ingredients. He discovered that he could successfully break the strict rules of the past and still produce high-quality food. Food is lighter, emphasis is on natural flavor rather than on rich sauces and hours of cooking. Though this simplification eliminates calories, the recipes are not strictly dietetic, as small amounts of butter, eggs, cream, fats, starches, and sugar can be used.

So, *cuisine minceur* is a new way of cooking which allows us to eat wisely and well. Heavy, ostentatiously rich food is a thing of the past. In essence, all excess is gone. We will be satisfied with our meals, but not uncomfortable or overstuffed.

To master *cuisine minceur*, it is necessary to learn a few basic principles and cooking techniques. Once you see how it works with the recipes included here you will also be able to adapt your favorite dishes to this new style of cooking or begin creating your own recipes.

The new cooking techniques are simple modifications of old methods, but preparation and cooking time is reduced, sometimes to a startling degree, and natural flavors and nutritional values are retained and enhanced.

Principles of
Cuisine Minceur

Here are ten principles of successful *cuisine minceur* cooking. As you will discover, there is nothing complicated about *cuisine minceur* methods. In fact, it is so natural that in a short while you will forget that you haven't always followed its precepts.

1. Use the freshest ingredients. Of course, if an ingredient is unavailable, frozen products can be substituted, but the result will be less satisfactory. Since it is rare to find fresh herbs all year round, I use some dried herbs in the recipes. If you are fortunate enough to have fresh herbs such as thyme, tarragon, basil, oregano, or dill, they should be used; double the amount given for the dried version in recipes. Parsley is available all year, so the amounts in the recipes are for fresh parsley. Meat, fish, and fruit must be fresh.

2. Butter, fats, cream, eggs, starches, and sugar are used only in minimum amounts. Rely on the natural sugar of fresh fruit when possible for a touch of sweetness.

3. Instead of thickening sauces with eggs, cream, or starches, sauces are thickened with puréed vegetables. Stocks or broths are reduced until thick. In some recipes

small amounts of ingredients such as *crème fraîche* (in this country a mixture of heavy and sour cream) are added at the last moment for the sauce to reach its peak. When cooking Chinese food, small amounts of arrowroot or cornstarch can be used.

4. Always trim off as much fat from meat as possible. If browning meat in small amounts of fat, remove meat and pat it dry with paper towels. The pan should be wiped clean of any fat with absorbent paper, too.

5. When cooking onions, garlic, leeks, or shallots or other vegetables in finely chopped state, use only a small amount of butter or oil and add a little white wine or sherry. This will release the vital juices and eliminate calories. If wine is not suitable for a particular dish, then use only a small amount of fat. A Teflon-coated pan helps here.

6. Cooking time in *cuisine minceur*, especially for vegetables, is short. Any fresh vegetable should be cooked in boiling water or stock until just tender crisp. Don't leave vegetables in pan in hot liquid. Remove and drain. Vegetables can be plunged into hot water for a minute before serving to revive and heat them.

7. There should be only two or three courses for lunch and three or four for dinner. Portions served should be moderate. Four to six ounces of meat per person is sufficient. There is no need for a meal to be meager, however. Make up for less meat by serving plenty of vegetables, salad, and fruit.

8. Presentation is extremely important to *cuisine*

minceur. A meal should be well-balanced and also attractive. Colors and flavors should blend beautifully.

9. Skim milk is used in all recipes requiring milk. If a richer result is desired, use a varying amount of nonfat dry milk dissolved in skim milk.

10. Be sure to read each recipe entirely before you begin to cook. This will enable you to have all ingredients on hand and know the amount of cooking time needed for a specific recipe.

Cuisine Minceur Cooking Techniques

BRAISING

Braising is an excellent cooking method for *minceur* cooking. The food is first browned in a small amount of fat and then cooked in liquid in a covered pot or casserole. Before the cooking liquid is added, the pan must be wiped clean of fat, and the food if possible should also be patted free of fat. Use a paper towel for this process. Braising will melt any fat on the meat, so fat should be trimmed off. Fat can be skimmed from the sauce at the end of the cooking time. It is easier to remove fat from sauce if the sauce is refrigerated. The fat solidifies and can be quickly removed.

COOKING IN ALUMINUM FOIL

Cooking in parchment paper is an ancient method. Foil is used in this book because it is readily available. When food is encased in foil, it cooks in its own juices and any flavoring that has been added. No butter is added to the food, but a tiny amount of butter is used to coat the foil to prevent cooked food from sticking.

FRYING

Frying is not an acceptable *cuisine minceur* method because so much fat is required for the cooking process.

MARINADES

Marinades are a great help to *cuisine minceur*. They enhance the flavor of a food and tenderize it. The marinades in this book are included in the recipes. However, creating marinades offers a great opportunity to do your own improvising. The longer a food is marinated, the more flavor it will have. Overnight is best.

POACHING

Poaching is a fine cooking method for *cuisine minceur*. It produces light, digestible food. The food is cooked completely immersed in water or other liquid. Place the food in the water when it is boiling, and cook over medium heat. Vegetables should be cooked quickly over medium heat. The liquid left from poaching is a good base for a stock. When a chicken or other food containing fat is cooked it will release the fat. This can be spooned off.

ROASTING

For *cuisine minceur*, roast meat or poultry can be browned in a little mixture of oil and butter on top of the stove in a frying pan before placing it in the oven. Then, the meat should be patted free of fat, leaving only a little on the surface to keep the meat from burning. The meat can be basted with a small amount of fat from time to time. Large birds can be wrapped in foil and cooked partially to prevent burning and then browned without the foil during the last part of the cooking time.

Poultry should be pierced over entire surface with point of knife or fork to release fat. However, don't pierce roast meat during cooking, for this would release vital juices and dry out the meat. Let roast meat rest before carving, and use the released juices for gravy. (See recipe for gravy under Sauces.)

SAUTÉING

For the new way to sauté, cook food in a small amount of oil and/or butter (about 1 tablespoon each usually will do) over high heat to brown. This is accomplished by using a skillet no larger than is absolutely necessary. The meat is removed and dried of fat with absorbent paper. The pan also should be wiped free of fat, but reserve the caramelized juices. Add wine or liquid to deglaze pan. Food is returned with other ingredients, covered, and cooked. A Teflon-coated pan also reduces the initial amount of fat needed.

STEAMING

With steaming, the food is cooked entirely by th
steam released from a boiling liquid, usually water. Th
food is placed on a rack over the liquid in a covered pot
In *cuisine minceur* a stock or bouillon can be used in
place of water to flavor the steaming food.

EQUIPMENT

A well-equipped kitchen is necessary for any kind of
cooking, but the only special equipment called for in
cuisine minceur that you may not already have is an
electric blender. Puréeing and blending are vital to this
cuisine. A food mill will accomplish some of the procedures, but not all.

A food processor is a great help to *cuisine minceur*,
but not essential. Stickproof or Teflon-coated pans are
helpful in *cuisine minceur* cooking, but they aren't vital.

I will mention here that good sharp knives, useful in
any style of cooking, are especially helpful for the slicing,
chopping, and dicing preparations that are necessary for
the new *minceur* cooking.

Menu Planning

A week of dinner menus *à la cuisine minceur* follows. I have selected balanced courses in terms of nutrition and presentation. They will, I hope, persuade you of the effectiveness of *minceur* eating. Lunch menus are not included because the family is rarely together at that time of day. However, any are suitable for lunch if it is the main meal of the day. If lunch is not the main meal, then use only two or three of the courses suggested, or select a salad from the many recipes in this book.

Twelve additional menus are offered so that you can substitute meals or mix them in with the other menus and have nearly a month of well-balanced meals without repeating the courses.

Week of
Cuisine Minceur
Dinner Menus

Monday   Melon with Lemon Mint Sauce
              Veal Ragout
              Purée of Baked Potatoes with Zucchini
              Orange and Lemon Snow

Tuesday   Vegetable Antipasto
              Boned Lamb Chops in Wine Sauce
              Spinach Salad with Pungent Yogurt
                 Dressing
              Fresh Pineapple with Mandarin Oranges
                 and Campari

Wednesday   Cold Asparagus with Vinaigrette *Minceur*
              Stuffed Flank Steak
              Baby Carrots in Curried *Crème Fraîche*
              Strawberry Sorbet Soufflé

Thursday   Mussels with Fresh Spinach and Vegetable
                 Stuffing
              Chicken Poached in Lemon Broth

Artichoke Hearts with Cucumbers
Sliced Oranges with Raspberry Sauce

Friday   Fresh Carrot Soup
Baked Red Snapper with Pernod in
   Aluminum Foil
Cauliflower on Eggplant Purée
Fresh Strawberries in *Crème Fraîche*

Saturday   Chicken Livers with Mushrooms and
   Cognac
Braised Duck
Vegetables in Iceberg Lettuce
Pears *Minceur*

Sunday   Marinated Grilled Shrimp with Tarragon
Cornish Game Hens Baked in Soy Sauce
Green Salad with Fresh Tomato Dressing
Baked Apples in Wine Sauce

More Menus:
A *Cuisine Minceur* Dozen

Zucchini Chowder
Tournedos of Beef with Onion Purée
Braised Fennel
Fresh Figs with Raspberries

Boiled Egg Whites with Ratatouille
Marinated Lamb Chops
Low-Calorie Caesar Salad
Blueberry Yogurt Dessert

Madrilène with Vegetable Garnish
Baked Striped Bass
Sautéed Cucumbers
Cherry Compote

Hearts of Palm and Asparagus Salad
Herbed Veal Chops with Garlic
Creamed Spinach
Almond Float with Fresh Fruit

Tomato Aspic
Chicken Normandy Style
Arugola and Endive Salad
Fresh Fruit with Lemon Sherbet

Chilled Pimiento Soup
Cold Trout with Mustard Sauce
Apples and Anchovies Salad
Fresh Fruit in Apricot Yogurt

Poached Bay Scallops
American Pot Roast *Minceur*
Vegetable Sauté
Fresh Peach and Plum Compote

French Onion Soup
Chicken Breasts *Classique*
Carrot Sticks with Béarnaise Sauce *Minceur*
Fresh Oranges in Spiced Wine Sauce

Mushrooms Stuffed with Tuna
Roast Veal Birds
Stewed Okra
Pineapple and Strawberry Ice

Shrimp Cocktail with Curried Cream Sauce
Navarin of Lamb
Watercress Salad
Lemon Sherbet

Buttermilk Borscht
Braised Lamb Shoulder
Broiled Tomatoes with Leeks
Honeydew Melon with Raspberries

Seafood Salad
Roast Capon with Mushrooms and Onions
Broccoli Mousse
Grilled Pineapple

Breakfast

It is important to begin each day with a meal that will give you energy. *Cuisine minceur* breakfasts are light, but they will provide you with necessary nutrients. Fresh fruit juice, a coddled, poached, or boiled egg (only one per person) or 2 ounces of low-fat cottage cheese with fresh cooked vegetable or raw fruit. *Cuisine minceur* includes no breads, but for a well-balanced diet one slice of unbuttered bread or toast is recommended. Serve coffee, tea, or bouillon piping hot.

For a special brunch or an extra-hearty breakfast, try Poached Eggs *à la bourguignonne*.

POACHED EGGS *À LA BOURGUIGNONNE*

4 rounded tablespoons hollandaise sauce *minceur* (See index for recipe)	½ bottle full-bodied red wine
	4 eggs
	4 thin slices toast

Bring wine to boil in 8″ frying pan. Gently drop eggs in pan 2 at a time and poach for 2 to 2½ minutes in simmering wine. Remove with slotted spoon and drain on absorbent paper. Place each egg on piece of toast with crusts trimmed, and top each with rounded tablespoon of hollandaise sauce *minceur*.

Garnish with fresh chopped parsley.

Serves 4.

Beverages

For *cuisine minceur* I recommend drinking fresh fruit drinks, skim milk, bouillon, tea, or coffee plain or with skim milk. Since liquor is fattening, it should be used in moderation. Only a glass or two of a light white or red wine with dinner is advised.

The three drink combinations that follow are favorites of mine. They can be served as a cocktail or a first course to any meal and are particularly refreshing for breakfast.

FRESH ORANGE AND STRAWBERRY DRINK

8 ounces freshly squeezed orange juice, well chilled

4 ripe strawberries, chilled

Purée ingredients in blender and serve with fresh mint leaves.

Serves 1.

TOMATO ORANGE DRINK

½ cup tomato juice, well
   chilled

½ cup freshly squeezed
   orange juice, well
   chilled

Combine ingredients in blender.

Serves 1.

TOMATO AND CLAM JUICE DRINK

½ cup tomato juice
½ cup clam juice

½ teaspoon
   Worcestershire sauce
dash of Tabasco sauce

Combine ingredients by stirring in pitcher. Serve hot
or cold.

Serves 1.

Appetizers

In *cuisine minceur* the number of courses is limited, so consider your appetizer as the first of only four courses at the most. Since the appetizer should never overwhelm what follows, be especially careful in selecting one that is just right to lead into the delicate *minceur* dishes.

BOILED EGG WHITE WITH RATATOUILLE

4 large hard-boiled eggs	1¼ cups ratatouille, chilled (See index for recipe)

Shell eggs and cut in half lengthwise. Remove egg yolks and use for another dish or discard. Spoon equal amounts of ratatouille into egg whites and serve on crisp bed of lettuce with black olives and cucumber sticks.

Serves 4.

BEEF TERIYAKI

½ cup soy sauce
2 teaspoons grated
    ginger root
2 scallions, grated

3 tablespoons dry sherry
2 pounds sirloin (1 inch
    thick), cut into strips
    ¼ inch by 2½ inches

Combine soy sauce, ginger root, scallions, and sherry. Add beef strips, toss, cover, and refrigerate for 1 hour. Thread on pieces of dampened wooden skewers and broil for 3 minutes. Brush with sauce and broil on other side 3 minutes more.

Serves 6 to 8.

BAKED MUSHROOMS STUFFED WITH TUNA

16 fresh mushrooms,
wiped clean

1 7-ounce can tuna
packed in water,
drained

3 tablespoons minced
celery

3 tablespoons minced
green pepper

1 tablespoon chicken
stock

1 tablespoon dry white
wine

1 tablespoon minced
scallion

¼ teaspoon dried
tarragon

¼ teaspoon dried
oregano

1 teaspoon fresh
chopped parsley

2 tablespoons grated
Parmesan cheese

Remove stems from mushrooms. Trim off ends, and chop stems fine. Place chopped stems and remaining ingredients, except for Parmesan cheese, in food processor or blender. Purée until smooth. Spoon filling into mushroom caps and sprinkle with grated Parmesan cheese. Place on baking sheet under broiler until top is lightly browned.

Serves 4.

CHICKEN LIVERS WITH MUSHROOMS AND COGNAC

1 cup beef broth
¼ cup dry red wine
¾ pound chicken livers
½ pound fresh mushrooms, wiped clean, stems trimmed and mushrooms quartered
2 tablespoons butter
1 tablespoon finely chopped shallots or scallions
salt and pepper to taste
½ teaspoon prepared mustard (Dijon-style best)
2 tablespoons Cognac
1 tablespoon freshly chopped parsley

In saucepan bring beef broth and red wine to a boil; add chicken livers and simmer for 5 minutes. Drain. Cut livers into small pieces and set aside. Bring 2 cups of lightly salted water to a boil and simmer mushrooms for 5 minutes. Drain. Melt butter in skillet and sauté shallots for 2 minutes. Add livers and mushrooms, and season with salt and pepper. Stir gently for a minute over medium-high heat. Add mustard and toss lightly. Pour in Cognac and cook for 2 more minutes. Sprinkle with parsley and serve immediately.

Serves 4.

CRABMEAT AND ARTICHOKE HEARTS

1 10-ounce package
  frozen artichoke
  hearts, cooked,
  chilled, and drained
6 ounces lump crabmeat,
  drained and
  separated
1 teaspoon grated lemon
  rind

½ cup black olives, cut
  into slivers
2 tablespoons minced
  pimiento
½ cup vinaigrette sauce
  minceur (See index
  for recipe)

Combine ingredients gently and serve on romaine lettuce leaves.

Serves 4.

CURRIED TUNA

2 7-ounce cans white
  meat tuna, packed in
  water, drained and
  flaked
1 tablespoon lemon juice
2 teaspoons curry
  powder
1 teaspoon sesame
  seeds

2 scallions, minced
2 teaspoons fresh
  chopped parsley
¼ cup mayonnaise
  minceur (See index
  for recipe)
2 tablespoons skim milk
  salt and freshly ground
  pepper to taste

Place ingredients in food processor and blend, or whip vigorously in bowl with fork.

Serve curried tuna in scooped-out cucumber boats or romaine lettuce leaves.

Serves 4 to 6.

MELON WITH SMOKED SALMON

8 thin slices cantaloupe
    or other melon
8 thin slices smoked

salmon
4 lemon wedges, seeded

On individual serving plates place 2 slices of melon. Top each with 2 slices smoked salmon and serve with lemon wedge.

Serves 4.

MARINATED GRILLED SHRIMP
WITH TARRAGON

1¼ pounds medium
    shrimp, shelled
    leaving tails intact
1 tablespoon lemon
    juice
1 tablespoon soy sauce
1 tablespoon dry
    sherry

2 tablespoons
    vegetable oil
1 teaspoon prepared
    mustard
1 teaspoon dried
    tarragon
1 teaspoon fresh
    chopped parsley
⅛ teaspoon freshly
    ground pepper

Combine all ingredients except for shrimp in bowl and mix. Then add shrimp, turn with spoon, cover, and marinate in refrigerator for 2 hours. Put shrimp on broiler rack and place 3 inches under heat of broiler for 2 minutes. Turn with tongs, brush with marinade, and cook until shrimps sizzle.

Serves 4.

MARINATED MUSSELS

2 pounds mussels,
  scrubbed clean and
  beards removed
¼ cup dry white wine or
  dry vermouth
¼ cup water
3 tablespoons olive oil
2 tablespoons lemon
  juice

3 tablespoons clam
  juice
1 teaspoon dry white
  wine
2 tablespoons fresh
  chopped parsley
2 cloves garlic,
  crushed
salt and freshly ground
  pepper to taste

Bring white wine and ¼ cup water to a boil in large pot. Add mussels, cover and cook over medium-high heat for 6 minutes. Remove mussels and tear off empty half of shell. Release mussels in shells with small knife and arrange on platter with pointed ends of shells facing away from center of plate. Place remaining ingredients in blender and purée. Spoon small amounts of marinade over mussels, cover, and leave at room temperature for at least 2 hours.

Serves 6 to 8.

MUSSELS WITH SPINACH AND TOMATO STUFFING

2 pounds mussels, scrubbed and beards removed
¼ cup dry vermouth
½ cup water
2 teaspoons vegetable oil
¼ cup finely chopped scallions
½ cup white wine
½ teaspoon dried oregano
½ teaspoon seasoned salt
½ cup finely chopped black olives
2 medium tomatoes, peeled and finely chopped
1 pound fresh spinach, washed, stems removed, dried and chopped fine
fresh grated Parmesan cheese

Bring vermouth and water to a boil in Dutch oven or large pot. Add cleaned mussels, cover, and cook over medium-high heat for 6 minutes. Drain. Tear off empty halves of shells and discard. Release each mussel in shell with sharp knife and leave in shell. Heat vegetable oil in skillet and sauté scallions for 2 minutes, stirring. Pour in wine and bring to a boil. Add remaining ingredients and cook, stirring, over medium-high heat until wine has evaporated and spinach has wilted, about 5 minutes. Spoon mixture in equal amounts over mussels in shells. Sprinkle lightly with grated Parmesan cheese and place under hot broiler about 3 inches from heat for 4 minutes or until topping sizzles.

Serves 6.

SHRIMP COCKTAIL WITH CURRIED CREAM DRESSING

16 large boiled shrimp, shelled, deveined and chilled
2 cups shredded lettuce
½ cup cream cheese *minceur* (See index for recipe)
3 tablespoons *crème fraîche* (See index for recipe)
1 teaspoon curry powder
1 tablespoon minced green pepper
1 tablespoon minced scallion
2 teaspoons fresh chopped parsley
1 tablespoon lemon juice
1 dash cayenne pepper salt and freshly ground pepper to taste

Divide lettuce on individual salad plates. Top each with 4 shrimps. Combine remaining ingredients in bowl and spoon over shrimp in equal amounts.

Serves 4.

SEVICHE

1 pound bay scallops
3 tablespoons lime juice
2 scallions, minced
1 tablespoon fresh
    chopped parsley

2 teaspoons olive oil
salt and freshly ground
    pepper to taste

Combine ingredients in bowl. Cover and refrigerate for 8 hours or overnight.

Serve on crisp lettuce leaves.

Serves 4.

STEAK TARTARE

1 pound lean beef
1 tablespoon capers
1 teasoon finely
    chopped parsley
2 teaspoons
    Worcestershire sauce
2 tablespoons finely
    chopped red onion

½ teaspoon prepared
    Dijon-style mustard
1 egg white
1 tablespoon vodka
salt and freshly ground
    pepper to taste

Place beef in bowl and make a well in the center of beef. Add all ingredients and mix thoroughly. Spread in thin layer on individual salad plates. Garnish with cornichons.

Serves 6 to 8.

VEGETABLE ANTIPASTO

2 fennel or celery sticks
2 raw cauliflower
    flowerets
2 black olives
2 green pepper strips

2 raw asparagus spears
2 cherry tomatoes
2 ¼-inch-thick slices
    cucumber
2 fresh mushrooms

Arrange vegetables on individual salad plate. Serve with vegetable dip. (See index for recipe).

Serves 1.

Soups and Stock

If you thought that only pure broth was permissible for a slimming meal, you are in for a delightful surprise. The variety of soups adapted to *minceur* cooking should suit the fussiest palate. Even the classic French onion is here—with fewer calories, of course.

Stocks are very important to any cuisine, as they are the basis for most soups and many sauces and gravies. Using your own prepared stock is especially important for *cuisine minceur* because it is carefully prepared to contain less fat. Stock is simple to make, and though it takes several hours of cooking, it doesn't need constant attention. Make it in large quantities and freeze it so that you will always have some on hand.

Commercially canned stocks are second best, although with the help of fresh vegetables, they can be made acceptable. A recipe is included for quick chicken stock. Bouillon cubes should never be used because their strong salty flavor will spoil any dish.

It is vital to remove all fats for *cuisine minceur*. Skim off the fat that rises to the surface from the beginning of the stock-making to the end. Fat should be removed from stock after refrigeration, too. The fat will rise to the surface and solidify, making final removal of all fat simple.

Stock may be kept in the regular part of the refrigerator two or three days, but it should be brought to a boil again before using. A richer stock is made by reducing it over heat until the desired strength is reached. This is called demi-glace sauce, and a recipe is included.

Stocks

BEEF STOCK

2 pounds beef bones, shin, shoulder or shank, cut into small pieces

2 pounds veal knuckle and bones, cut into small pieces

3 carrots, scraped and chopped

2 medium onions, chopped

2 shallots, minced

2 stalks celery, chopped

2 tomatoes, peeled, seeded, and cut into wedges

2 tablespoons tomato paste

bouquet garni (3 sprigs parsley, ¼ teaspoon thyme, 1 bay leaf, and 6 peppercorns tied in cheesecloth of double thickness)

1 cup dry white wine

3½ quarts cold water

Place beef and veal bones, carrots, onion, shallots, and celery in roasting pan. In preheated 450 F. oven brown ingredients for about 15 minutes, turning often. Drain off any fat. Transfer browned ingredients to large pot with remaining ingredients. Bring to a boil, immediately reduce heat, and simmer for about 3 hours. Skim fat and scum from surface occasionally. Strain, cool, cover, and refrigerate. After refrigeration, remove rest of fat from surface.

Yield: about 1½ quarts.

DEMI-GLACE SAUCE

Demi-glace sauce is a concentrated beef stock. It is made by simmering stock until reduced by half, skimming as necessary.

Demi-glace can be used to deglaze the pan after any meat has browned in it. This dissolves caramelized juices in the pan, which are vital to flavor. Reduced, it makes a delicious sauce.

PAN GRAVY

In roasting pan, caramelized juices have accumulated after roasting meat. Remove roast and pour off almost all fat. Add double the amount of hot water or stock you wish to end up with. Bring to a boil and stir with spoon until caramelized juices dissolve. Boil until reduced by half. Taste for seasoning. Stir in a tablespoon of butter at final moment to finish sauce.

CHICKEN STOCK

4 pounds chicken carcasses, wings, backs, or necks

2 pounds veal shank and knuckle, split

2 leeks, roots trimmed and about 2 inches of green left, sliced lengthwise and washed well

3 carrots, scraped and sliced

2 stalks celery, quartered.

1 tablespoon finely chopped shallots

1 medium onion, halved

1 bouquet garni (3 sprigs parsley, ½ teaspoon thyme, 1 bay leaf, and 6 peppercorns tied in double thickness of cheesecloth)

1 cup dry white wine

5 quarts cold water

2 teaspoons salt

Place all ingredients in large stockpot. Bring to a boil, immediately reduce heat, and simmer for about 3 hours. Skim fat and scum as it rises to surface.

Strain stock, cool, cover, and refrigerate. Remove fat that rises to surface and solidifies. Use amount desired and freeze the rest.

Makes about 3 quarts.

QUICK CHICKEN STOCK

4 cups canned chicken
   stock
1 cup cold water
½ cup dry white wine
1 carrot, scraped and
   chopped

1 stalk celery, chopped
1 medium onion,
   chopped
⅛ teaspoon dried thyme
3 sprigs parsley
1 small bay leaf

Place ingredients in pot and bring to a boil, reduce heat immediately, and simmer about 45 minutes. Strain, cool, cover, and refrigerate. Remove any fat on surface.

Makes about 3 cups.

COURT BOUILLON

1¼ quarts water
1 cup dry white wine
1 stalk celery, chopped
1 onion, chopped
1 carrot, scraped and
   sliced
1 bay leaf

2 ¼-inch-thick slices
   lemon
6 peppercorns
3 sprigs parsley
1 teaspoon salt

Place ingredients in saucepan and bring to boil. Reduce heat and simmer for 25 minutes. Strain through fine mesh strainer.

Yield: 1½ quarts.

FISH STOCK

2 pounds fish bones and heads
1 medium onion, chopped
1 stalk celery, chopped
1 leek (white part only) cleaned and chopped
¼ teaspoon dried thyme
1 bay leaf
3 sprigs of parsley
1 quart water
1 cup dry white wine
¼ teaspoon salt, or to taste

Place ingredients in saucepan and bring to a boil. Reduce heat and simmer for 45 minutes. Strain through fine mesh strainer.

Yield: 1 quart.

Soups

BUTTERMILK BORSCHT

1 16-ounce can diced
   beets (save ½ cup
   beet juice)
4 scallions, chopped
2 tablespoons lemon
   juice
1 medium tomato,
   peeled, seeded, and
   chopped

1 quart buttermilk
   salt and freshly
   ground pepper to
   taste
3 carrots, peeled, diced,
   and cooked
   chopped chives

Place beets, scallions, lemon juice, tomato, and beet juice in food processor or blender and purée. Pour into large bowl, and add buttermilk. Season with salt and pepper. Chill for at least 4 hours.

Garnish with diced carrots and chives.

Serves 6.

CHILLED PIMIENTO SOUP

1 cup pimientos,
   drained
2 cups vegetable or
   chicken stock
1½ cups tomato juice
2 tablespoons lemon
   juice

1 teaspoon soy sauce
2 dashes Tabasco
   sauce
salt and freshly
ground pepper to
taste

Purée ingredients in blender and chill thoroughly. Garnish with diced cucumber.

Serves 4.

COLD CUCUMBER SOUP

2 cups plain yogurt
1 medium cucumber,
  peeled and grated
1 teaspoon lemon juice
¼ teaspoon dried mint

1 teaspoon sugar
1 cup cold club soda
  salt and freshly ground
  white pepper to taste

Combine ingredients and chill well in refrigerator. Stir before serving.

Garnish with diced green pepper.

Serves 4.

FRENCH ONION SOUP

3 tablespoons vegetable
oil
3 large onions, thinly
sliced
1 tablespoon flour
2 quarts beef stock
4 tablespoons dry sherry
1 teaspoon lemon juice

salt and pepper to
taste
4 1-inch-thick slices
toasted French bread
2 tablespoons freshly
grated Parmesan
cheese

Heat oil in Dutch oven. Over very low heat sauté onions, stirring often, for about 25 minutes. Sprinkle in flour and mix. Add beef stock, sherry, and lemon juice. Season with salt and pepper. Bring to a boil, reduce heat to a simmer, and cook for 20 minutes. Divide soup equally between 4 ovenproof soup bowls and top with a slice of toasted French bread. Sprinkle with equal amounts of cheese. Place under broiler until cheese is lightly browned.

Serves 4.

FRESH CARROT SOUP

2 teaspoons butter
1 stalk celery, chopped
1 medium onion, chopped
1 pound carrots, scraped and sliced
1 tomato, peeled and chopped
¼ teaspoon dried thyme
1 quart chicken stock
salt and freshly ground pepper to taste
1 teaspoon fresh chopped chives

Melt butter in saucepan. Add celery and onions and cook, stirring, for 3 minutes. Add remaining ingredients except for chives. Bring to a boil, reduce heat, and simmer for 25 minutes. Purée in blender a few cups at a time and strain. Serve in warmed soup bowls garnished with fresh chopped chives.

Serves 6.

FRESH TOMATO SOUP

1 teaspoon vegetable oil
4 ripe tomatoes, peeled
   and chopped
2 teaspoons finely
   chopped shallots
1 medium onion,
   chopped
2 tablespoons tomato
   paste

¼ teaspoon dried thyme
½ teaspoon dried basil
1 bay leaf, crumbled
1 quart chicken stock
   salt and freshly ground
     pepper to taste

Heat oil in sauce pan. Add tomatoes, shallots, and onion. Cook, stirring, for 5 minutes. Add remaining ingredients and bring to a boil, reduce heat, and simmer for 25 minutes. Discard bay leaf. Purée in blender and strain. Check seasoning.

Garnish with freshly chopped parsley.

Serves 4.

FRESH VEGETABLE SOUP

1 tablespoon butter	2 potatoes, peeled
2 tablespoons dry white wine	1 cup shredded cabbage
2 carrots, scraped	¾ cup fresh green peas
2 stalks celery	1½ quarts chicken stock
2 leeks, white part only	salt and freshly ground pepper

Cut vegetables into thin julienne strips. Melt butter in heavy pot with wine. Add carrots, celery, leeks, potatoes, and cabbage. Cook over medium heat for 2 minutes, stirring. Add green peas, stock, salt, and pepper. Bring to a boil, reduce heat, and simmer for 15 minutes or until vegetables are tender.

Serves 6.

GAZPACHO

2 cups tomato juice
4 medium tomatoes,
  peeled and seeded
3 scallions, chopped
1 clove garlic, minced
1 small green pepper,
  seeded and chopped
1 medium cucumber,
  peeled and chopped

2 tablespoons lemon
  juice
1 tablespoon vegetable
  oil
½ teaspoon salt, or to
  taste
freshly ground pepper
  to taste

Combine ingredients in large bowl. Purée in blender several cups at a time. Check seasoning, and chill well before serving. Accompany with little bowls filled with diced tomato, green pepper, onion, and cucumber to be spooned on soup as garnish.

Serves 4.

MADRILÈNE WITH VEGETABLE GARNISH

2 10-ounce cans
  madrilène or jellied
  consommé, well
  chilled
2 scallions, minced
2 stalks celery,
  minced

1 small green pepper,
  minced
6 water chestnuts,
  minced
4 teaspoons lemon juice
1 teaspoon dried mint

Divide madrilène or consommé into 4 bowls and chill. Combine remaining ingredients in small bowl. Spoon mixture over madrilène or consommé when ready to serve.

Serves 4.

MUSHROOM SOUP

2 tablespoons butter
1 pound mushrooms,
    wiped clean, stems
    trimmed
3 cups skim milk
1 cup milk made with

½ cup nonfat dry
milk powder and
1 cup water
salt and freshly ground
pepper to taste

Chop mushrooms coarsely. Heat butter in saucepan and sauté mushrooms and scallions for 3 minutes, stirring. Add 3 cups skim milk and bring to a boil, reduce heat, and simmer for 10 minutes. Add nonfat dry milk and continue heating for 5 minutes, stirring frequently. Season with salt and pepper. Purée in blender a few cups at a time. Check seasoning.

Garnish with fresh chopped parsley and watercress leaves.

Serves 4.

OKROSCHKA

3 cups skim milk
1 cup plain yogurt
2 scallions, minced
1 medium cucumber,
   peeled and diced
2 stalks celery, diced
1 dill pickle, diced

1 cup diced cooked
   shrimp
1 cup diced cooked
   chicken breast meat
1 tablespoon white wine
   vinegar
salt and freshly ground
   pepper to taste

Combine milk and yogurt in bowl. Add remaining ingredients. Cover and refrigerate for several hours. Check seasoning before serving. Sprinkle with fresh chopped parsley.

Serves 6 to 8.

SPINACH SOUP

1 pound fresh spinach,
   washed, stemmed,
   and dried
salt and pepper
dash or two of nutmeg
2 teaspoons butter
1 tablespoon dry white
   wine

1 clove garlic, crushed
1 tablespoon finely
   chopped shallots
2 cups chicken stock
1 cup skim milk with
   ¼ cup nonfat dry
   milk added

Steam spinach over boiling water for 5 minutes. Remove and chop. Season with salt, pepper, and nutmeg. Heat butter in saucepan with wine. Add garlic and shallots and cook, stirring, for 2 minutes. Add remaining ingredients and bring to a boil, reduce heat, and simmer for 15 minutes. Purée in blender a few cups at a time. Reheat, adding a little more milk if mixture is too thick. Check seasoning.

Serves 4.

VICHYSSOISE *MINCEUR*

2 tablespoons vegetable
   oil
4 leeks, roots trimmed
   and all but 2 inches
   of leaves cut off,
   root split and washed,
   thinly sliced

3 medium potatoes,
   peeled and thinly
   sliced
1 teaspoon salt
3 cups skim milk
3 cups chicken stock
   fresh chopped chives

Heat vegetable oil and sauté leeks over medium heat
for 5 minutes. Stir occasionally. Add remaining ingredients and bring to a boil. Reduce heat to a simmer,
partially cover, and cook for 40 minutes. Check seasoning. Purée in blender a few cups at a time or force
through food mill. Strain. Chill thoroughly.

Garnish with fresh chopped chives.

Serves 6.

WATERCRESS SOUP

1 tablespoon butter
1 tablespoon dry white
    wine or dry vermouth
2 leeks, white parts only,
    well washed
1 clove garlic, crushed
1 potato, peeled and
    finely diced

1 quart chicken stock
½ teaspoon salt
1 bunch watercress,
    washed, stemmed,
    and chopped
freshly ground pepper
    to taste

Melt butter with white wine in large saucepan. Add leeks and garlic. Cook for 3 minutes, stirring. Add potatoes, stock, and salt. Bring to a boil, reduce heat, and simmer for 15 minutes. Add watercress and pepper to taste. Simmer for 10 minutes more. Purée in blender a few cups at a time. Check seasoning.

Serves 4 to 6.

ZUCCHINI CHOWDER

1 tablespoon butter
1 pound zucchini, peeled
   and diced
2 carrots, diced
1 medium onion, finely
   chopped
1 clove garlic, crushed
½ teaspoon dried thyme
2 cups chicken stock

2 cups skimmed milk
   into which ½ cup
   nonfat dry milk has
   been dissolved
1 7-ounce can minced
   clams
salt and freshly ground
   pepper to taste

Melt butter in saucepan. Add zucchini, carrots, onion, and garlic, and cook over medium heat for 5 minutes, stirring. Add thyme, stock, and skim milk mix, and season with salt and pepper. Bring to a boil, reduce heat, and simmer for 20 to 25 minutes until vegetables are tender. Purée in blender or force through food mill a few cups at a time. Return soup to clean saucepan and add clams. Heat thoroughly.

Garnish with fresh chopped parsley.

Serves 6.

Salad Dressings and Sauces

Cuisine minceur dressings are made with little or no oil. Salads will often require a little more in quantity than regular oil dressings, because the substitute ingredients do not coat the salad ingredients as easily.

Cream cheese *minceur* and *crème fraîche*, which are used in many *minceur* recipes, are not dressing sauces. They have been included in this section for the sake of convenience.

CREAM CHEESE *MINCEUR*

2 cups low-fat creamed cottage cheese

¼ cup plain yogurt

Place cottage cheese and yogurt in food processor or blender, and purée until mixture is very smooth. There must not be any lumps in mixture. Cover and refrigerate for 8 hours before cheese can be used.

Yield: about 2 cups.

CRÈME FRAÎCHE

1 cup heavy cream   1 cup sour cream

Place heavy and sour cream in a glass jar with a lid. Shake vigorously and cover. Leave at room temperature 10 hours. Stir at this point, re-cover, and refrigerate for one day before using. *Crème fraîche* will keep for about seven days in the refrigerator.

Yield: 2 cups.

ANCHOVY AND GARLIC DRESSING

½ cup vinaigrette sauce *minceur* (See index for recipe)
1 large clove garlic, crushed

2 anchovy fillets (soaked in milk for 10 minutes and patted dry), chopped fine

Whisk together all ingredients, cover, and chill for an hour before serving. Whisk again just before serving on salad or other food.

Yield: ½ cup.

HERB DRESSING

1 tablespoon vegetable oil
2 tablespoons red wine vinegar
¼ cup chicken stock
¼ teaspoon dried tarragon
½ teaspoon fresh chopped chives
½ teaspoon fresh chopped dill
1 teaspoon fresh chopped parsley
½ tomato, peeled, seeded, and chopped
salt and pepper to taste

Place all ingredients in blender and purée.

Yield: About ½ cup.

LEMON DRESSING

1 tablespoon vegetable oil
1 tablespoon lemon juice
½ teaspoon grated lemon rind
3 tablespoons yogurt
salt and pepper to taste

Combine ingredients with wire whisk.

Yield: about ⅓ cup.

ORANGE DRESSING

½ cup orange sections
1 tablespoon minced
  scallions
1 tablespoon lemon
  juice
1 teaspoon sugar
1 teaspoon vegetable oil
1 ripe medium tomato,
  peeled and seeded
salt and freshly ground
  pepper to taste

Purée ingredients in blender and taste for seasoning.

Yield: about ¾ cup.

MUSTARD DRESSING

3 tablespoons chicken
  stock
1½ tablespoons
  vegetable oil
1 teaspoon prepared
  mustard
½ teaspoon fresh
  chopped chives
salt and freshly
  ground pepper to
  taste

Whisk ingredients together in small bowl with wire whisk and serve immediately, or whisk just before serving.

Yield: about ⅓ cup.

SPICY TOMATO DRESSING

cup tomato juice

teaspoon
Worcestershire sauce

2 scallions, minced

medium tomato,
peeled, seeded, and
chopped

1 clove garlic, crushed

1 tablespoon lemon juice

½ teaspoon Dijon-style
mustard

2 dashes Tabasco sauce
salt and freshly ground
pepper to taste

Purée ingredients in blender until smooth. Chill 1 hour
before serving.

Yield: about 1 cup.

THOUSAND ISLAND DRESSING

2 tablespoons red wine
vinegar

cup low-fat creamed
cottage cheese

1 tablespoon minced
green pepper

1 dill pickle, minced

2 tablespoons minced
red onion

2 tablespoons tomato
paste

2 tablespoons plain
yogurt

1 teaspoon finely
chopped parsley
salt and freshly ground
pepper to taste

Combine ingredients in bowl and chill well before
serving.

Yield: about 1 cup.

VINAIGRETTE SAUCE *MINCEUR*

3 tablespoons chicken
  stock
1 tablespoon vegetable
  oil
1½ tablespoons red wine
  vinegar or lemon
  juice

½ teaspoon dry
  mustard
salt and freshly
  ground pepper to
  taste

Combine ingredients in small bowl with wire whisk and serve immediately, or whisk just before serving.

Yield: about ⅓ cup.

Since it is quite impossible to make mayonnaise, hollandaise, or béarnaise sauce without doing it according to the classic recipes, I have invented a way to extend a thinning mayonnaise recipe into the two delicious sauces. However, they contain an egg yolk and oil, so they must be used in small portions.

BASIC MAYONNAISE *MINCEUR*

1 egg yolk, room
  temperature
⅛ teaspoon salt
  freshly ground white
  pepper to taste
1 teaspoon prepared
  Dijon-style mustard

4 tablespoons vegetable
  or olive oil
½ teaspoon white wine
  vinegar
3 tablespoons cream
  cheese *minceur* (See
  index for recipe)

Whisk together yolk, salt, pepper, and mustard. With the whisk, slowly beat in oil drop by drop until sauce thickens. Drop by drop, beat in white wine vinegar. Fold in cream cheese *minceur*.

Yield: about ⅔ cup.

HERBED MAYONNAISE

½ cup mayonnaise
minceur

1 tablespoon finely
chopped fresh parsley

½ teaspoon dried
tarragon

1 tablespoon finely
chopped fresh
watercress

salt and freshly ground
pepper to taste

Combine ingredients and refrigerate for several hours before serving.

Yield: about ¾ cup.

MAYONNAISE *MINCEUR* WITH FENNEL

½ cup mayonnaise
  minceur
3 tablespoons chopped
  fennel

1 teaspoon fresh
  chopped parsley
salt and freshly ground
  pepper to taste

Combine ingredients and chill well before using.
Serve with poached or grilled fish.

Yield: about ¾ cup.

BÉARNAISE SAUCE *MINCEUR*

⅔ cup mayonnaise
  minceur
4 tablespoons red wine
  vinegar
3 tablespoons minced
  shallots

1½ teaspoons dried
  tarragon
1 teaspoon fresh
  chopped parsley
salt to taste

In saucepan heat vinegar, shallots, and tarragon. Salt
to taste. Simmer for about 4 minutes until a little less
than 1 tablespoon of vinegar remains. Cool completely.
Mix with parsley into mayonnaise *minceur* which has
been prepared to the point of adding cream cheese
minceur. After adding shallot mixture, fold in 3 tablespoons cream cheese *minceur*. Sauce must be served at
room temperature.

Yield: about ¾ cup.

HOLLANDAISE SAUCE *MINCEUR*

Prepare mayonnaise *minceur*, but whisk in 2 tea-spoons lemon juice, drop by drop, in place of white wine vinegar, and fold in 4 instead of 3 tablespoons cream cheese *minceur*. Sauce must be served at room temperature.

Yield: about ¾ cup.

HORSERADISH SAUCE

2 tablespoons white horseradish
½ cup cream cheese *minceur* (See index for recipe)
1 teaspoon lemon juice
salt and freshly ground pepper to taste
1 tablespoon skim milk

Combine ingredients well. Check seasoning.

Yield: a little over ¾ cup.

MINT SAUCE

1 cup demi-glace sauce
   (See index for
   recipe)
1 tablespoon fresh
   chopped mint or 1
   teaspoon dried mint

1 tablespoon tarragon
   vinegar
1 teaspoon sugar

Place ingredients in saucepan and heat over very low heat for 10 minutes. Do not boil.

Yield: 1 cup.

MUSHROOM SAUCE

2 tablespoons finely
   chopped shallots
¼ teaspoon dried thyme
1 cup beef stock
1 teaspoon fresh
   chopped parsley

¼ cup mushroom
   purée (See index for
   recipe)
1 teaspoon lemon juice
salt and freshly ground
   pepper to taste

Bring shallots, thyme, and stock to a boil in a small heavy saucepan. Reduce heat, and simmer for 15 minutes. Strain. In clean pan heat liquid and add parsley, mushroom purée, and lemon juice. Season with salt and pepper.

Yield: about ¾ cup.

PEACH SAUCE

6 ripe fresh peaches,
   peeled, pitted, and
   quartered, or
   16-ounce can
   unsweetened peach
   halves, drained*

⅔ cup water
2 tablespoons sugar, or
   to taste
1 teaspoon kirsch

Place ingredients in saucepan and simmer for 15 minutes, stirring frequently. Purée in blender, and check taste. Refrigerate sauce until ready to use.

Yield: about 1 cup.

*Or substitute 10 to 12 ripe apricots or 16-ounce can unsweetened apricot halves, drained.

RAITA

1 medium cucumber,
   peeled
   salt
1 cup plain yogurt

1 teaspoon sugar
freshly ground pepper
   to taste

Grate cucumber and place in colander. Sprinkle with salt, and leave in sink to drain for 30 minutes. Mix cucumber with remaining ingredients and refrigerate for 2 hours before serving.

Yield: 1 cup.

SAUCE VERTE

½ cup low-fat creamed
   cottage cheese
2 tablespoons chicken
   stock
¼ cup cooked chopped
   spinach
¼ cup chopped
   watercress

½ teaspoon dried
   tarragon
1 scallion, minced
2 tablespoons red wine
   vinegar
salt and freshly ground
   pepper to taste

Purée ingredients in blender. Check seasoning. Chill thoroughly before serving.

Yield: about 1 cup.

SEAFOOD COCKTAIL SAUCE

½ cup tomato sauce
   minceur or canned
   tomato sauce
1 tablespoon lime juice
1 teaspoon
   Worcestershire sauce

dash Tabasco sauce
1 tablespoon grated
   onion
1 teaspoon horseradish
salt and freshly ground
   pepper to taste

Combine ingredients and chill thoroughly before serving.

Yield: about ¾ cup.

STEAK SAUCE

2 medium-large ripe
  tomatoes, peeled and
  seeds removed
1 tablespoon
  Worcestershire sauce
1 tablespoon lemon
  juice
2 teaspoons prepared
  mustard
salt and freshly ground
  pepper to taste

Chop tomatoes and place all ingredients in blender. Purée until smooth, and check seasoning.

Yield: about 1 cup.

TOMATO SAUCE *MINCEUR*

8 plump ripe tomatoes, peeled, seeded, and chopped
1 tablespoon vegetable oil
2 tablespoons dry white wine or dry vermouth
2 cloves garlic, minced
1 medium onion, finely chopped
3 cups chicken stock
½ teaspoon dried basil
½ teaspoon dried oregano
1 bay leaf
2 tablespoons tomato paste
1 tablespoon Bovril
salt and freshly ground pepper to taste

Purée tomatoes in food processor or force through food mill. Heat oil and wine in large saucepan, and sauté garlic and onion for 5 minutes, stirring occasionally. Add remaining ingredients, including tomato purée, and stir. Heat over medium-low heat for 30 minutes, stirring often. Cook until reduced to nice thickness, and check seasoning.

Yield: about 3 cups.

VEGETABLE DIP

2 cups low-fat creamed cottage cheese
3 tablespoons minced celery
2 scallions, minced
½ cup minced pimiento
1 tablespoon soy sauce
1 tablespoon lemon juice
½ teaspoon dried basil
2 dashes Tabasco
salt and freshly ground pepper to taste

Combine ingredients and refrigerate for a few hours. Serve with fresh vegetables such as cucumber slices, carrot sticks, or raw asparagus spears.

Yield: about 3 cups.

Salads

If meat is the heart of a meal, then salad is the soul.
n enticing and beautifully presented salad will en-
ven any *minceur* menu.

Be sure to use the special *minceur* dressings and
auces where indicated. They are all in the preceding
ection, but check the index for the exact page.

APPLES WITH ANCHOVIES

2 Delicious apples,
peeled, cored, and
diced
4 anchovies (soaked in
skim milk for 10
minutes and patted
dry), finely chopped

1 tablespoon raisins
⅓ cup mayonnaise
minceur, or as needed

Combine ingredients and chill well before serving.

Excellent served with cold striped bass or roast
hicken.

Serves 4.

ARUGOLA AND ENDIVE SALAD

1 fresh bunch arugola, stems trimmed, washed, and dried

3 endives, leaves separated, washed, dried, and cut in half

2 tablespoons olive oil

1 tablespoon lemon juice

2 tablespoons chicken stock or water

1 finely chopped shallot

½ teaspoon Dijon-style mustard

salt and freshly ground pepper

Put arugola and endive into salad bowl. Combine remaining ingredients in blender and purée. Pour over salad. Toss.

Serves 4.

BROCCOLI SALAD

1 large bunch of fresh
   broccoli, stem ends
   trimmed and leaves
   removed
¾ cup vinaigrette sauce
   minceur (See index
   for recipe)

1 clove garlic, crushed
2 teaspoons fresh
   chopped parsley

Cook broccoli in large pot in ½ inch of lightly salted boiling water, covered, until tender crisp, about 8 minutes. Drain. When cool enough to handle, quarter each stalk and gently place in bowl. Add garlic and parsley to sauce vinaigrette *minceur* and mix. Pour sauce over broccoli, cover, and refrigerate for several hours.

Serves 4.

CANTALOUPE WITH LEMON MINT SAUCE

2 cantaloupes, halved
   and seeds removed
½ cup vinaigrette sauce
   minceur
1 tablespoon lemon juice

1 teaspoon chopped
   fresh mint or ½
   teaspoon dried mint
¼ cup cream cheese
   minceur

Combine vinaigrette sauce *minceur*, lemon juice, mint, and cream cheese *minceur* with whisk. Spoon in equal amounts into center of melons.

Garnish with fresh mint leaves.

Serves 4.

CANTALOUPE, CABBAGE, AND APPLE SALAD

1 small cantaloupe,
   peeled and seeded
1½ cups shredded
   cabbage
2 Golden Delicious
   apples, peeled,
   cored, and sliced
   thin

1 cup plain yogurt
1 tablespoon sugar
1 teaspoon lemon juice
½ teaspoon poppy
   seeds

Slice cantaloupe and cut into 1-inch pieces. Place in salad bowl with cabbage and apples. Mix remaining ingredients in small bowl and pour over salad. Toss and chill for 2 hours.

Serves 4 to 6.

CAULIFLOWER SALAD

2 cups raw cauliflower, broken into small flowerets and pieces

1 16-ounce can large black olives, pitted and halved

½ pint cherry tomatoes, halved

2 scallions, minced

½ cup lemon dressing *minceur* (See index for recipe)

Combine cauliflower, black olives, cherry tomatoes, and scallions in salad bowl. Pour dressing over vegetables and toss.

Serves 4.

CHEF SALAD *MINCEUR*

1 quart mixed lettuce
   pieces
½ pound lean roast
   beef, cut into thin
   strips
½ pound boiled tongue,
   cut into thin strips
1 large boiled chicken
   breast, skinned,
   boned, and cut into
   thin strips

2 tomatoes, cut into
   wedges
1 green pepper, seeded
   and cut into thin
   strips
1 cup cooked beets, cut
   into thin strips
1 cup vinaigrette sauce
   minceur

Divide mixed lettuce into 4 individual salad bowls.
Arrange remaining ingredients, except for dressing, over
lettuce in equal amounts. Pour ¼ cup of dressing over
each salad.

Serves 4.

ESCAROLE AND GRAPEFRUIT SALAD

1 small head escarole, washed, dried, and broken into bite-sized pieces

2 carrots, scraped and shredded

1 cup grapefruit sections, drained

½ cup vinaigrette sauce *minceur*

½ teaspoon sugar

Combine pieces of escarole, carrots, and grapefruit in salad bowl. Add sugar to vinaigrette sauce. Pour sauce over salad and toss.

Serves 4.

CHICKEN AND FRESH MUSHROOM SALAD

2 chicken breasts,
  boiled
½ cups thinly sliced
  mushrooms
2 tablespoons lemon
  juice
1 tablespoon soy
  sauce
½ cup cream cheese
  minceur

½ teaspoon dried
  tarragon
1 teaspoon fresh
  chopped chives
salt and freshly
  ground pepper to
  taste
1 tablespoon fresh
  chopped parsley

Skin and bone chicken, and cut into thin slices. Place in bowl with mushrooms. Purée remaining ingredients in blender, and pour over chicken and mushrooms. Combine and chill well before serving.

Serves 4.

FENNEL SALAD

1 cup sliced fennel

1 medium cucumber, peeled, seeded, and sliced

1 cup halved cherry tomatoes

1 small red onion, thinly sliced

1 cup shredded iceberg lettuce

1 tablespoon fresh chopped parsley

½ cup vinaigrette sauce *minceur*

Combine salad ingredients in bowl. Pour sauce over salad and toss.

Serves 4 to 6.

GREEN BEAN AND TOMATO SALAD

pound fresh green
   beans, cooked,
   chilled, and cut into
   1-inch lengths

2 medium-large
   tomatoes, peeled and
   cut into wedges

½ teaspoon dried basil

1 tablespoon red wine
   vinegar

2 tablespoons chicken
   stock

¼ cup low-calorie
   cottage cheese

¼ teaspoon salt
   freshly ground pepper
   to taste

Put green beans and tomatoes in salad bowl. Place remaining ingredients in blender and purée. Pour dressing over salad and toss.

Serves 4.

GREEN SALAD WITH FRESH TOMATO DRESSING

1 head Boston lettuce, washed, dried, and torn into bite-sized pieces

1 cucumber, peeled and thinly sliced

Fresh Tomato Dressing:

1 tablespoon vegetable oil

2 tablespoons red wine vinegar

2 thin slices yellow onion

2 whole medium-sized ripe tomatoes, peeled and seeded

½ teaspoon dried basil salt and freshly ground pepper to taste

Place ingredients in blender and purée until mixture is quite smooth. Check seasoning and gently toss with lettuce and cucumbers.

Serves 4.

HEARTS OF PALM AND ASPARAGUS
SALAD

1 13-ounce can hearts of palm, drained and cut into 1-inch lengths

0 stalks cooked asparagus, cut into 1-inch lengths

1 tablespoon chopped pimiento

1 teaspoon capers

1 teaspoon finely chopped parsley

2 tablespoons vegetable oil

2 tablespoons lemon juice

2 tablespoons water

1 tablespoon chopped scallions

salt and freshly ground pepper

Combine hearts of palm and asparagus pieces, pimiento, capers, and parsley in bowl. Blend remaining ingredients in blender and pour over salad. Toss gently and chill well before serving.

Serves 4.

LOW-CALORIE CAESAR SALAD

1 medium head romaine
   lettuce
1 tablespoon vegetable
   oil
1 clove garlic, crushed
2 tablespoons lemon
   juice
1 egg white, boiled for
   1 minute in shell with
   yolk (discard yolk)

1 tablespoon
   Worcestershire sauce
3 tablespoons chicken
   stock
6 anchovy fillets
   (soaked in skim milk
   for 10 minutes and
   patted dry), chopped
salt and freshly ground
   pepper to taste

Break lettuce into bite-sized pieces and place in salad bowl. In small bowl combine oil, garlic, lemon juice, egg white, Worcestershire sauce, and chicken stock. Pour this mixture over salad and toss. Sprinkle anchovies over salad and toss again. Season to taste with salt and pepper.

Serves 4.

MANHATTAN SALAD

¼ pound medium
 boiled shrimp,
 shelled, deveined,
 and coarsely chopped
2 dozen cocktail onions
1 large tomato, peeled,
 seeded, and diced
1 tablespoon capers
½ cucumber, peeled,
 seeded, and chopped

1 tablespoon lemon
 juice
2 tablespoons vegetable
 oil
¼ teaspoon dry mustard
 salt and pepper to
 taste
Boston lettuce leaves

Place chopped shrimp, onions, chopped tomato, and capers in bowl. Purée cucumber, lemon juice, and oil seasoned with dry mustard, salt and pepper in blender. Check seasoning. Add a little water if necessary to make smooth purée. Pour over shrimp mixture. Cover and refrigerate for 2 hours.

Serve on Boston lettuce leaves.

Serves 4.

MARINATED ARTICHOKE HEARTS

1 10-ounce package
frozen artichoke
hearts, cooked and
drained

1 tablespoon vegetable
oil

2 tablespoons chicken
stock

2 tablespoons red wine
vinegar

1 tablespoon capers

1 tablespoon finely
chopped shallots

1 small clove garlic,
crushed

½ teaspoon prepared
mustard

2 tablespoons minced
pimientos

1 teaspoon fresh
chopped parsley

salt and freshly ground
pepper to taste

Combine ingredients in bowl, cover, and refrigerate
for several hours before serving.

Serves 4.

ORANGE AND BEET SALAD

4 cooked beets, sliced   ½ cup vinaigrette sauce
3 oranges, sliced   *minceur*

Arrange beets and oranges alternately on salad platter.
Pour sauce over all, cover, and chill thoroughly.

Serves 4.

ORANGE, CUCUMBER, AND CELERY SALAD

2 navel oranges, peeled,   3 stalks celery, sliced
   all white membrane   ½ cup orange dressing
   removed and oranges   *minceur* (See index
   cut into sections   for recipe)
1 large cucumber,
   peeled and sliced

Combine orange sections, cucumber slices, and celery
in salad bowl. Pour dressing over all and toss.

Serves 4.

POTATO SALAD

5 medium potatoes,
  cooked and peeled
½ cup white wine vinegar
1 small green pepper,
  seeded and diced
3 scallions, minced
½ teaspoon celery seeds

1 teaspoon prepared
  mustard
1 teaspoon finely
  chopped parsley
½ teaspoon salt
freshly ground pepper
  to taste

While potatoes are still warm, place in bowl and pour vinegar over them. Toss gently. Add remaining ingredients and combine. Check seasoning.

Serves 4 to 6.

ROAST RED PEPPER AND TOMATO SALAD

2 red peppers
3 medium ripe tomatoes, sliced
2 tablespoons red wine vinegar
1 tablespoon tomato paste
½ teaspoon paprika
½ teaspoon dried basil
1 clove garlic, crushed
4 tablespoons chicken stock
1 tablespoon vegetable oil
salt and freshly ground pepper to taste

Roast red peppers under hot broiler until skin has blackened on all sides. Remove skin, remove seeds, and core. Cut into thin strips and place in bowl with tomatoes. In another bowl add remaining ingredients and mix well. Pour over peppers and tomatoes and toss. Cover and refrigerate for two hours before serving.

Serves 4.

SALAD LARA

1 tablespoon capers
2 tablespoons chopped
cocktail onions
2 tablespoons chopped
dill pickle
½ cup button
mushrooms, chopped
3 tablespoons red wine
vinegar
½ teaspoon dry mustard
¼ cup tomato juice

½ teaspoon dried
tarragon
1 teaspoon fresh
chopped parsley
salt and freshly ground
pepper to taste
8 slices of cucumber
about ¼ inch thick
4 medium ripe red
tomatoes, peeled and
cut in half lengthwise

Combine capers, onions, pickle, and mushrooms with vinegar, mustard, tomato juice, tarragon, parsley, salt, and pepper. Arrange cucumbers on flat serving dish. Top each cucumber with half a tomato with cut side down. Pour dressing mixture over tomatoes, cover, and refrigerate for 2 hours.

Serves 4.

SALADE NIÇOISE

1 medium head romaine
  lettuce, washed,
  dried, and broken
  into bite sized pieces
1 cucumber, peeled
  and sliced
2 tomatoes, cut into
  wedges
1 small green pepper,
  seeded and cut into
  thin strips

½ pound cooked green
  beans
12 pitted black olives
1 7-ounce can white
  meat tuna, packed in
  water and drained
1 tablespoon capers
⅔ cup vinaigrette sauce
  minceur (See index
  for recipe)

Place lettuce in salad bowl and arrange remaining ingredients, except for dressing, over lettuce. Pour dressing over salad and toss.

Serves 4.

SALMON SALAD

½ pound smoked salmon, cut into thin strips

1 cup cooked fresh or frozen green peas

3 cooked carrots, diced

1 boiled potato, diced

1 tablespoon fresh chopped parsley

1 teaspoon fresh chopped chives

½ cup mayonnaise *minceur* (See index for recipe)

salt and freshly ground pepper to taste

Gently fold salmon, peas, carrots, and potato together with parsley, chives, mayonnaise, salt, and pepper. Serve on crisp bed of lettuce.

Serves 4.

SEAFOOD SALAD

1 cup cooked lobster
meat, cut into
bite-sized pieces

1 cup cooked shrimp,
shelled, deveined,
and coarsely chopped

5 ounces crabmeat,
separated

5 black olives, pitted
and cut into slivers

1 teaspoon capers

2 tablespoons finely
chopped fennel

1 teaspoon finely
chopped chives

1 tablespoon lemon
juice

½ cup mayonnaise
minceur (See index
for recipe)

Combine ingredients well, and chill for several hours before serving. Serve with cold cooked asparagus.

Serves 4.

SPINACH AND MUSHROOM SALAD WITH SPICY TOMATO DRESSING

1 pound fresh spinach, washed, stemmed, dried, and broken into bite-sized pieces

½ pound fresh mushrooms, wiped clean and thinly sliced

¾ cup spicy tomato dressing, *minceur* (See index for recipe)

Place spinach and sliced mushrooms in salad bowl. Pour dressing over salad and toss.

Serves 4.

SPINACH SALAD WITH PUNGENT YOGURT DRESSING

1 pound fresh spinach, washed, stems trimmed, dried, and broken into bite-sized pieces
6 fresh asparagus spears

16 snow pea pods, stems and thread along length of pods removed.
6 fresh mushrooms, thinly sliced

Yogurt Dressing:

¾ cup plain yogurt
2 tablespoons soy sauce
½ tablespoons lemon juice
¼ teaspoon seasoned salt
¼ teaspoon salt
¼ teaspoon freshly ground pepper
2 scallions, finely chopped

In a 10-inch skillet bring to boil 1 inch of lightly salted water. Add asparagus and simmer for 8 minutes. Drain and cool. Drop cleaned snow pea pods into saucepan with enough boiling water to cover, and cook for 3 minutes. Drain. Cut asparagus and snow pea pods into four sections each. Place spinach, asparagus, snow pea pods, and mushrooms in salad bowl and refrigerate until well chilled. In small bowl mix yogurt dressing ingredients with small whisk. Check seasoning. Pour over salad and toss.

Serves 4.

TOMATO ASPIC

2 envelopes plain gelatin
4 cups tomato juice
1 tablespoon
  Worcestershire sauce

1 tablespoon lemon juice
2 dashes Tabasco

Soften gelatin in ¼ cup cold water. Heat 2 cups tomato juice and stir in softened gelatin until completely dissolved. Add remaining ingredients. Pour into lightly oiled 1-quart mold and chill until firm.

Serves 6.

WATERCRESS SALAD

1 bunch watercress,
washed, dried, and
stems cut off

1 8-ounce can mandarin
oranges, drained

12 endive leaves, washed,
dried, and cut into
bite-sized pieces

⅓ cup orange juice

1 tablespoon lemon juice

1 tablespoon vegetable
oil

¼ teaspoon dry mustard
salt and pepper to
taste

Break watercress into bite-sized pieces and place in salad bowl with mandarin oranges and endive. In small bowl mix together remaining ingredients. Pour over watercress salad and gently toss.

Serves 4.

VEGETABLE SALAD

1 scallion, minced
1 cup fresh or frozen
  peas, cooked
3 carrots, scraped, diced,
  and cooked
1 large baking potato,
  peeled, cooked, and
  diced

½ teaspoon dried basil
¾ cup Thousand Island
  dressing *minceur*
  (See index for
  recipe)

Combine scallion, peas, carrots, potato, and basil in bowl. Pour dressing over vegetables and gently toss. Serve on romaine lettuce leaves.

Serves 4.

Vegetables

With vegetables, more is less. Serve at least two, and the absence of starch will not seem overwhelming.

ARTICHOKE HEARTS AND CUCUMBERS

1 10-ounce package frozen artichoke hearts
1 large cucumber, peeled
salt and freshly ground pepper to taste
2 teaspoons finely chopped parsley
1 tablespoon lemon juice
2 teaspoons butter

Cook artichoke hearts according to package directions. Meanwhile, cut cucumber in half lengthwise and scrape out seeds with teaspoon. Slice cucumbers in ½-inch pieces. Drop in lightly salted boiling water and cook for 6 minutes. Drain artichoke hearts and cucumber. Place in bowl with remaining ingredients and toss. Check seasoning.

Garnish with fresh chopped parsley.

Serves 4.

ASPARAGUS WITH VINAIGRETTE *MINCEUR*

20 asparagus spears   ¾ cup vinaigrette sauce
                                    minceur (See index
                                    for recipe)

Cut off tough ends of asparagus. With sharp small knife peel the stalks. Gently lower asparagus into 3 quarts of lightly salted boling water and cook about 7 minutes or until just tender crisp. Remove and drain. Place in serving dish and pour vinaigrette sauce *minceur* over asparagus. Refrigerate for several hours before serving.

Serves 4.

ARTICHOKES WITH HOLLANDAISE
SAUCE *MINCEUR*

4 large fresh artichokes
salt

1 cup hollandaise sauce
  minceur (See index
  for recipe)

Trim off stems of artichokes and remove tough outer
leaves. Cut off top of center leaves with sharp knife.
With scissors cut off tops of all leaves. Bring 3½
quarts of lightly salted water to a boil in pot and place
artichokes in water, stem ends down. Simmer for about
40 minutes, depending on size of artichokes. Test for
doneness by piercing stem end of artichokes with sharp
point of knife to see if they are tender. Drain well and
cool. Refrigerate and serve cold with ¼ cup of hollandaise
sauce *minceur* for each individual.

Serves 4.

BRAISED CABBAGE

3 cups shredded
  cabbage
2 teaspoons butter
1 tablespoon finely
  chopped shallots

⅔ cup dry white wine
  salt and freshly ground
  pepper to taste

Melt butter in saucepan. Add shallots and cook for two minutes, stirring. Add remaining ingredients, cover, and cook for about 12 minutes, or until cabbage is tender.

Serves 4.

BABY CARROTS IN CURRIED *CRÈME FRAÎCHE*

2 cups chicken stock
1 pound baby carrots, stems removed, scraped
1 tablespoon white wine vinegar
1 teaspoon curry powder

salt and freshly ground pepper to taste
1 teaspoon fresh chopped parsley
3 tablespoons *crème fraîche* (see index for recipe)

Bring chicken stock to a boil in saucepan. Add carrots and cook for 7 to 8 minutes, or until just tender crisp. Drain and reserve stock. Combine 2 tablespoons stock, wine vinegar, and curry powder in small bowl, then add to carrots. Season with salt and pepper. Gently toss and cool. Sprinkle with parsley and *créme fraiche*. Toss and serve at room temperature.

Serves 4.

BRAISED FENNEL

2 full bulbs fennel
2 cloves garlic, crushed
1½ cups chicken stock

salt and pepper to taste

Cut off stem ends of fennel and remove outer leaves. Wash well and cut in half lengthwise. Pour chicken stock with garlic into frying pan and bring to a boil. Add fennel and season with salt and pepper. Simmer, covered, until tender, about 20 minutes.

Serves 4.

BRAISED CELERY HEARTS

2 celery hearts
1 onion, quartered
1 carrot, scraped and
  sliced

2 cups chicken broth
salt and pepper to
taste

Trim off ends of stalks of celery. Cut each heart bunch in half lengthwise. Cut each half in half. Rinse off any dirt. Place celery on bottom of baking dish with onion and carrot, then pour in broth. Cover and bake in pre-heated 350° F. oven for 1 hour. Remove celery to warm serving dish. Strain liquid in baking dish and season with salt and pepper. Spoon several tablespoons of seasoned liquid over celery and serve.

Serves 4.

BRAISED LEEKS

4 leeks, roots trimmed
and all but 2 inches
of leaves cut off
1 tablespoon finely
chopped shallots

1 cup chicken stock
salt and freshly ground
pepper to taste

Cut leeks in half lengthwise and wash under cold running water to remove all dirt and sand. Arrange leeks with shallots in large skillet and pour stock over all. Season with salt and pepper. Cover and simmer leeks for about 15 minutes, or until tender.

Serves 4.

BROCCOLI MOUSSE

1 large bunch cooked
  broccoli spears
1 teaspoon Dijon-style
  mustard
¾ cup mayonnaise
  minceur (See index
  for recipe)
1 tablespoon finely
  chopped scallions
2 tablespoons cream
  cheese *minceur* (See
  index for recipe)

2 teaspoons lemon juice
  salt and freshly ground
  pepper to taste
1 envelope plain gelatin
  softened in small sauce
  pan in ½ cup cold
  water and heated over
  low heat
3 egg whites

Purée cooked broccoli in food processor or blender
a few chopped stalks at a time. Place in bowl with
mustard, mayonnaise *minceur*, scallions, cream cheese
minceur, lemon juice, dissolved gelatin, and salt and pepper to taste. Combine. Whip egg whites until stiff peaks
form, and fold into mixture. Pour into lightly oiled 1½-
quart mold and chill until set.

Serves 6.

BRUSSELS SPROUTS AND CARROTS

1 pint frozen Brussels
  sprouts.
3 carrots, scraped and
  thinly sliced
2 tablespoons minced
  onion

¾ cup chicken stock
  salt and freshly ground
    pepper to taste
1 tablespoon fresh
  chopped parsley

Par-boil Brussels sprouts for 15 minutes. Place all ingredients except for parsley in saucepan. Bring to a boil, reduce heat to a simmer, cover, and cook for 10 minutes. Sprinkle with parsley.

Serves 4.

BROILED TOMATOES WITH LEEK STUFFING

1 large leek, white part
  only, finely chopped
1 cup chicken stock
2 large ripe tomatoes
½ teaspoon dried basil

1 teaspoon vegetable oil
  salt and freshly ground
  pepper to taste
2 teaspoons dried bread
  crumbs

In small saucepan bring stock to a boil. Add finely chopped leeks, and cook for about 8 minutes until tender. Strain. Place leeks in bowl. Cut tomatoes in half crosswise. Scoop out pulp and add pulp to cooked leek with basil, oil, salt and pepper to taste. Mix well. Fill tomato half with mixture in equal portions. Sprinkle with bread crumbs. Place on baking sheet 3 or 4 inches under heated broiler until top turns golden.

Serves 4.

CARROT STICKS WITH BÉARNAISE SAUCE *MINCEUR*

1 pound carrots, scraped
   and cut into sticks 1½
   inch long and ⅓ inch
   wide

2 cups chicken stock
⅓ cup béarnaise sauce
   minceur (see index
   for recipe)

In saucepan, bring stock to a boil. Cook carrots over medium heat for 8 minutes or until tender crisp. Drain and place in serving dish. Add béarnaise sauce *minceur* Toss.

Serves 4.

CAULIFLOWER ON EGGPLANT PURÉE

1 medium eggplant,
    peeled and cubed
2 teaspoons butter
2 tablespoons dry white
    wine
1 tablespoon finely
    chopped shallots
1 tablespoon minced
    green pepper
salt and freshly ground
    pepper

1 small cauliflower,
    separated into
    flowerets and cooked
    in simmering
    water until tender
    crisp, drained
1 teaspoon fresh
    chopped parsley

Cook eggplant in 2 cups of lightly salted boiling water until tender, about 5 minutes. Drain. Place eggplant in bowl and stir vigorously with fork, making purée. Heat butter with wine in saucepan and add green pepper. Stir over medium heat for 3 minutes. Add eggplant and season with salt and pepper. Cook, stirring, for about 5 minutes, to reduce moisture. Place in shallow serving dish just large enough to comfortably hold mixture and top with cauliflower stems ends down. Sprinkle with parsley.

Serves 4.

CREAMED SPINACH

2 pounds fresh spinach
  or 2 10-ounce
  packages frozen
  chopped spinach
  salt
3 tablespoons dry white
  wine
2 tablespoons finely
  chopped shallots

½ cup cream cheese
  minceur (See index
  for recipe)
few grates of fresh
  nutmeg
salt and freshly ground
  pepper to taste

Clean and stem spinach. Steam over salted boiling water for 5 minutes (cook frozen spinach according to package directions). Drain spinach and force out as much water as possible by pressing spinach in strainer with the back of a spoon. If fresh spinach is used, chop it coarsely. In saucepan heat wine and add shallots. Cook over medium-high heat until wine is reduced to 1 tablespoon. Add spinach, cream cheese *minceur*, nutmeg, salt, and pepper. Mix well. Stir over heat until heated through.

Serves 6.

ITALIAN SPINACH

1 tablespoon olive oil
2 cloves garlic, minced
1 small onion, minced
½ cup chicken stock
2 pounds fresh spinach,
washed, stemmed, dried,
and chopped
pinch freshly grated
nutmeg
½ teaspoon dried basil

salt and freshly ground
pepper to taste
3 anchovy fillets, soaked
in milk to cover for
10 minutes, dried,
and chopped
1 tablespoon freshly
grated Parmesan
cheese, or to taste

Heat olive oil in skillet, and sauté garlic and onion for 3 minutes. Add stock, spinach, nutmeg, basil, salt and pepper to taste. Stir, cover, and cook for about 6 minutes over medium heat. Add anchovies and Parmesan cheese, stir, re-cover, and cook for 1 minute. Test seasoning.

Serves 6.

MUSHROOM PURÉE

1 pound mushrooms,
  wiped clean and
  stems trimmed
2 teaspoons lemon juice
1 cup skim milk
1 teaspoon butter

1 tablespoon finely
  chopped shallots
salt and freshly ground
  pepper to taste
1 teaspoon fresh
  chopped parsley

In saucepan heat butter and sauté shallots for 3 minutes. Add milk and bring to a boil. Add mushrooms, which have been quartered, and cook over medium heat for 5 minutes. Strain, reserving liquid. Purée mushrooms in food processor or blender until smooth. Add a little of the liquid as needed to result in creamy purée.

Yield: about 1 cup.

ONION PURÉE

5 medium onions,
  peeled and chopped
2 cups chicken stock
1 clove garlic, minced

salt and freshly ground
  pepper to taste
1 teaspoon lemon juice

Bring stock to a boil. Add onions, garlic, salt, and pepper. Simmer for about 20 minutes until tender. Drain and reserve stock. Purée onions in food processor or blender and add lemon juice. Purée. Place purée in small saucepan and cook over medium heat, stirring, for about 5 minutes to eliminate some of moisture from mixture.

Yield: about 1 cup.

POACHED ZUCCHINI

3 medium-size zucchini	2 tablespoons fresh
4 cups water	chopped parsley
1 teaspoon salt	

Peel zucchini. Cut each in half lengthwise. Then cut the halves in half lengthwise. With small sharp knife, cut away pulp with seeds in center of zucchini and shape pieces of zucchini into 1 inch ovals by trimming away corners of each piece. Drop into boiling, salted water and cook for 8 minutes. Drain and place in bowl. Sprinkle with parsley. Season lightly with salt and pepper. Toss lightly and serve immediately.

Serves 4 to 6.

For variety, sprinkle with 2 tablespoons grated Parmesan cheese and toss.

PURÉED ARTICHOKES

2 10-ounce packages
   frozen artichoke
   hearts*
1 tablespoon lemon juice
2 dashes cayenne pepper

salt and freshly ground
   pepper to taste
3 tablespoons cream
   cheese *minceur* (See
   index for recipe)

Cook artichoke hearts according to package directions and drain. Place in food processor or blender with lemon juice, cayenne pepper, salt and pepper, and cream cheese *minceur*. Purée. Check seasoning.

Serves 6.

*Frozen artichoke hearts are used in this recipe and others because they have excellent flavor and are easier to prepare than large fresh artichokes.

PURÉED CARROTS

1 pound carrots, scraped
  and sliced
1 onion, halved
2 cups chicken stock
¼ teaspoon dried thyme
1 bay leaf

½ teaspoon salt
  freshly ground pepper
  to taste
2 tablespoons *crème
  fraîche* (See index
  for recipe)

In saucepan bring stock, onion, thyme, bay leaf, salt
and pepper to a boil. Add carrots and simmer for 2
minutes until tender. Drain and discard onion and bay
leaf. Purée carrots in food processor or blender with
crème fraîche.

Serves 4.

PURÉED CAULIFLOWER

1 large head cauliflower,
   separated into
   flowerets
3 cups skim milk
1 leek, white part only,
   chopped

1 clove garlic, crushed
   salt and freshly ground
    pepper to taste

In saucepan bring skim milk to a boil. Add cauliflower, leek, garlic, and salt and pepper. Simmer for 20 minutes, strain, and reserve liquid. Purée cauliflower and leek in food processor or blender. Add a little of liquid the cauliflower cooked in, if necessary.

Serves 4.

PURÉED GREEN PEAS

2 cups fresh green peas
  or 1½ 10-ounce
  packages frozen
  green peas
2 cups chicken stock
1 teaspoon butter

salt and freshly ground
  pepper to taste
2 tablespoons *crème
  fraîche* (See index
  for recipe)

In saucepan bring stock to a boil. Add peas and cook
until tender. Drain, reserving liquid, and purée in food
processor or blender with butter and *crème fraîche*. Season with salt and pepper. If necessary, add a little reserved liquid.

Serves 4 to 6.

RATATOUILLE

1 medium-large onion,
  cut into 1 inch
  slivers
3 tablespoons dry white
  wine
1 medium eggplant,
  peeled and cubed
3 tomatoes, peeled and
  cubed
2 medium zucchini,
  cubed

1 small green pepper,
  seeded and chopped
½ teaspoon dried basil
½ teaspoon dried
  oregano
1 bay leaf
1 cup chicken stock
salt and pepper to taste

Place white wine and onions in large saucepan and
bring to a boil. Cook until wine is reduced to 1 tablespoon. Add remaining ingredients and bring to a boil.
Reduce heat and simmer for 40 minutes, covered.

Serves 6.

STEWED OKRA

1 pound fresh okra,
  stems trimmed
2 teaspoons butter
1 teaspoon oil
1 medium-large onion,
  chopped fine
2 cloves garlic, minced

5 ripe tomatoes, peeled,
  seeded, and chopped
½ teaspoon cumin
½ teaspoon dried basil
½ teaspoon salt
freshly ground pepper
  to taste

In skilet, heat butter with oil. Sauté onion and garlic for 3 minutes, stirring. Add all other ingredients, cover, and simmer for about 18 minutes until okra is tender.

Serves 4 to 6.

SAUTÉED CUCUMBERS

2 large cucumbers, peeled	1 teaspoon vegetable oil
salt and freshly ground pepper to taste	1 teaspoon fresh chopped parsley
2 teaspoons butter	

Cut cucumbers in half. Scoop out seeds with teaspoon. Cut cucumbers in half lengthwise again and slice into 1 inch pieces. With small sharp knife shape into ovals. Drop into lightly salted boiling water to cover, and cook for 5 minutes. Drain. Melt butter with oil in skillet and add cucumbers. Sauté over high heat, shaking pan occasionally to turn cucumbers, until lightly browned. Season with salt and pepper, and sprinkle with parsley.

Serves 4.

VEGETABLE SAUTÉ

1 pound fresh
  mushrooms
2 tablespoons vegetable
  oil
2 tablespoons dry white
  wine
½ cup chicken stock
½ cup chopped green
  beans

½ cup diced carrots
½ cup diced celery
1 cup shredded cabbage
1 cup fresh or frozen
  green peas
salt and freshly groune
  pepper to taste

Wipe mushrooms clean and remove stems. Chop ste
fine. Heat oil in skillet, and add chopped stems a
sauté for 5 minutes, stirring. Add remaining ingredien
including halved mushroom caps, cover, and cook ov
low heat for 25 minutes.

Serves 6.

VEGETABLES BAKED IN ICEBERG LETTUCE

6 fresh broccoli spears
2 carrots, scraped and diced
¼ pound fresh string beans, trimmed and chopped into ¼-inch lengths
2 teaspoons butter

2 tablespoons finely chopped shallots
⅔ cup dry white wine
salt and freshly ground pepper to taste
4 large iceberg lettuce leaves

Steam broccoli spears for 10 minutes and drain. Cook carrots in 2 cups slow-boiling water for 5 minutes and drain. Cook chopped green beans in simmering water for 8 minutes. Drain. Chop broccoli and combine with carrots and green beans. In skillet melt butter and sauté shallots for 2 minutes, stirring constantly. Add ⅓ cup wine and cook, stirring for 1 minute over high heat. Remove from heat and mix with vegetables. Season with salt and pepper to taste. Bring 2 quarts of lightly salted water to a boil. Add lettuce leaves and simmer for 3 or 4 minutes. Remove lettuce leaves carefully and spread out each leaf on paper towel. Trim off 1 inch of thick center rib of each lettuce leaf. Spoon equal amounts of vegetable mixture into center of each lettuce leaf and bring sides of lettuce up over filling. Place leaves, folded side down, in lightly buttered small shallow baking dish. Pour in remaining wine. Cover dish with lightly buttered foil. Bake in preheated 350° F. oven for 20 minutes.

Serves 4.

Seafood

Foil baking is one of the main secrets involved in making a fish dish delicate and completely, deliciously *minceur*.

BAKED HALIBUT WITH CLAM SAUCE

4 ¾-inch thick halibut steaks (4 to 6 ounces each)
½ cup fish stock or bottled clam juice
½ cup dry white wine
1 scallion, chopped
½ cup minced cooked clams, cooled
1 teaspoon lemon juice
1 tablespoon parsley
3 tablespoons *crème fraîche* (See index for recipe)
salt and freshly ground pepper to taste

Place halibut steaks in shallow baking dish. Heat stock, wine, and scallion in saucepan and pour over fish. Cover with lightly buttered pieces of foil and bake in preheated 375° F. oven for 20 minutes. Meanwhile, combine chopped clams, lemon juice, parsley, and *crème fraîche*. Season to taste with salt and pepper. Carefully remove fish with spatula to warmed serving dish. Spoon sauce over fish.

Serves 4.

BAKED POMPANO WITH VEGETABLES

4 pompano fillets
  salt and freshly ground
    pepper
2 teaspoons minced
    onion
2 ripe tomatoes, peeled
    and chopped

½ teaspoon dried basil
1 tablespoon lemon juice
    dash Tabasco
1 tablespoon melted
    butter

Season fillets with salt and pepper. Place on lightly greased baking dish. In bowl combine onion, tomatoes, basil, lemon juice, Tabasco, and butter. Spread mixture in equal portions over fillets. Place in preheated 375° F. oven and bake for about 20 minutes.

Serves 4.

BAKED RED SNAPPER WITH PERNOD
IN ALUMINUM FOIL

1 tablespoon butter

4 ¼-inch thick slices
of large yellow onion

2 teaspoons fresh
chopped dill or 1
teaspoon dried
dillweed

4 6-ounce fillets of red
snapper

salt and freshly ground
pepper

4 tablespoons Pernod

½ cup fish stock or clam
broth

paprika

Cut 4 aluminum foil ovals large enough to comfortably hold each fish fillet. Rub butter over inside of each foil oval. Place onion slice on foil. Sprinkle with dill, and top with snapper fillet. Turn foil up to catch liquid. Season with salt and pepper, and spoon a fourth of the Pernod and fish stock over each fillet. Sprinkle with paprika. Seal foil by folding edges together. Place on baking sheet in preheated 350° F. oven and bake for 25 minutes.

Serves 4.

BAKED STRIPED BASS

1 3½-to-4-pound
  striped bass, cleaned
1 cup diced carrots
1 cup chopped fennel
1 medium onion,
  chopped
½ teaspoon dried
  tarragon
  salt and freshly ground
  pepper

½ cup dry white wine
1 fresh ripe tomato,
  peeled and chopped
  fine
3 tablespoons *crème
  fraîche* (See index
  for recipe)

Season fish inside and out with salt and pepper. On sheet of lightly buttered aluminum foil large enough to comfortably hold fish, arrange carrots, fennel, and onion. Sprinkle with tarragon and salt and pepper, and top with fish. Turn foil up to catch liquid. Pour wine over fish, and seal edges of foil together. Place foil in roasting pan and cook in preheated 375° F. oven for about 40 minutes or until fish is done. With two spatulas carefully remove fish to heated platter. Strain juices in foil and pour over fish. Mix vegetables with chopped tomato and *crème fraîche*. Season and serve with fish.

Serves 4.

BROILED MARINATED SWORDFISH STEAKS

4 6-ounce swordfish
   steaks
2 teaspoons vegetable
   oil
2 tablespoons soy sauce
1 tablespoon lemon juice
½ cup dry white wine

¼ teaspoon dried
   tarragon
3 tablespoons minced
   scallions
salt and freshly ground
   pepper to taste

Place steaks in shallow baking dish. Combine remaining ingredients. Pour over fish. Turn steaks, cover, and
refrigerate for 2 hours. Broil steaks 3 or 4 inches from
heat for about 12 minutes until fish browns lightly. Serve
with lemon wedges.

Serves 4.

CHILLED LOBSTER SALAD

3 cups cooked lobster
   meat, cut into
   bite-sized pieces
½ teaspoon dried
   tarragon
2 teaspoons lemon juice

⅔ cup mayonnaise
   minceur (See index
   for recipe)
2 teaspoons fresh
   chopped parsley
salt and freshly ground
   pepper to taste

Place lobster in bowl and sprinkle with tarragon and lemon juice. Toss. Add mayonnaise *minceur*, parsley, and season with salt and pepper. Toss and chill thoroughly before serving.

Serve on crisp lettuce leaves with sliced tomatoes and cornichons.

Serves 4.

COLD STRIPED BASS WITH *SAUCE VERTE*

1 3½-to-4-pound
    striped bass
6 cups court bouillon
  (See index for recipe.)

1 cup *sauce verte* (See
    index for recipe)

Wrap fish in cheesecloth and place in roasting pan, and pour court bouillon over fish. Cover pan with aluminum foil, place in preheated 350° F. oven, and cook for about 25 minutes or until done. Carefully remove fish to serving dish and chill for several hours. Remove cheesecloth, and skin fish with sharp point of a small knife. Decorate platter with watercress or parsley and lemon wedges, and serve with *sauce verte* in sauceboat.

Serves 4.

COLD FILLET OF SOLE WITH
SALMON MAYONNAISE

4 fillets of sole (4 to 6
    ounces each)
salt and freshly ground
    pepper to taste
½ cup dry white wine
¼ cup fish stock or
    bottled clam juice
1 slice onion
1 teaspoon lemon juice
2 sprigs parsley
6 ounces cooked
    salmon, flaked

1 teaspoon capers
1 teaspoon finely
    chopped parsley
½ cup mayonnaise
    minceur (See index
    for recipe)
4 large iceberg lettuce
    leaves
4 slices ripe tomato
    mayonnaise minceur

Season sole fillets with salt and pepper. In saucepan, bring wine, fish stock or clam juice, onion, lemon juice, and parsley sprigs to a boil. Place fillets in lightly buttered dish just large enough to hold fish and pour ingredients from saucepan over fish. Cover with foil and place in preheated 375° F. oven for 15 minutes. Mean-

American Cuisine Minceur Cookbook — 89-456-G

while, in bowl combine salmon, capers, parsley, and ½ cup mayonnaise minceur. Set aside. Poach lettuce leaves in boiling water for 2 minutes, drain, and spread on absorbent paper. Carefully remove fillets. Spread equal amounts of salmon mixture over fillets and fold in half. Place each fillet in center of lettuce leaf and wrap. Cover and chill thoroughly. At serving time top each lettuce-wrapped fillet with a slice of tomato and a dollop of mayonnaise minceur.

Garnish with lemon wedge.

Serves 4.

MUSSELS *MARINIÈRE*

2 pounds mussels, scrubbed and beards removed
1 tablespoon olive oil
2 cloves garlic, crushed
1 onion, chopped
1 stalk celery, diced
1 carrot, scraped and diced
½ teaspoon dried thyme
½ teaspoon dried tarragon
1 bay leaf
1 cup dry white wine
salt and freshly ground pepper to taste
1 tablespoon fresh chopped parsley

Heat olive oil in large pot and sauté garlic, onion, celery, and carrot for 3 minutes, stirring. Add herbs, bay leaf, and wine. Bring to a boil and cook for 10 minutes. Strain and return liquid to cleaned pot. Bring to a boil again, add mussels, cover, and cook for 6 minutes. Place mussels in individual bowls and pour liquid over mussels. Sprinkle with parsley.

Serves 4.

COLD TROUT WITH MUSTARD DRESSING

4 rainbow trout,
cleaned
6 cups court bouillon

(See index for
recipe)

Mustard Sauce:

2 teaspoons Dijon-style
mustard
2 tablespoons cream
cheese *minceur* (See
index for recipe)
2 tablespoons *crème*

fraîche (See index
for recipe)
1 teaspoon fresh
chopped parsley
salt and freshly ground
pepper

Place trout in roasting pan just large enough to comfortably hold fish. Pour court bouillon over trout. Cover with lightly buttered foil, place in preheated 350° F. oven, and poach for 20 minutes. Let trout cool, then chill in refrigerator in poaching liquid. Meanwhile, prepare sauce by combining remaining ingredients. Carefully remove trout with two spatulas, and with point of small sharp knife remove skin of each trout on upper side. Surround with parsley, and serve with mustard sauce.

Serves 4.

POACHED BAY SCALLOPS

1 pound bay scallops
1 cup dry white wine
1 cup fish stock or
   bottled clam juice
2 sprigs parsley
1 bay leaf

salt and freshly ground
   pepper to taste
2 tablespoons lemon
   juice
¾ cup *sauce verte* (See
   index for recipe)

Bring white wine, stock or clam juice, parsley, and bay leaf to a boil. Add scallops, and season lightly with salt and pepper. Cook for 4 minutes. Drain and discard parsley and bay leaf. Place scallops in dish and sprinkle with lemon juice. Cover and chill thoroughly.

Serve scallops in Boston lettuce leaves with *sauce verte*.

Serves 4.

POACHED SALMON STEAKS

4 1-inch-thick salmon
   steaks (4 to 6 ounces
   each)
  salt and freshly ground
   pepper to taste
4 slices onion

½ cup dry white wine
½ cup fish stock or
   bottled clam juice
3 sprigs parsley
1 teaspoon lemon juice

Season salmon with salt and pepper. Place onion, white wine, stock, parsley, and lemon juice in skillet. Bring to a boil, add salmon, cover, and simmer for 15 minutes. Carefully remove salmon to dish. Strain liquid in pan, and pour over salmon. Cover and cool in refrigerator.

Serve with mayonnaise *minceur* with fennel and lemon wedges.

Serves 4.

SALMON STEAKS BAKED IN FOIL

4 1-inch salmon steaks
   salt and freshly ground
     pepper to taste
½ cup fish stock or
   bottled clam juice

4 teaspoons lemon juice
   freshly chopped
     parsley

Season salmon steaks with salt and pepper. Place each in sheet of lightly buttered aluminum foil. Turn foil up to catch liquid. Spoon 2 tablespoons fish stock and 1 teaspoon lemon juice over each steak, and enclose in foil by sealing edges together. Place in preheated 350° F oven and bake for 25 minutes. Slit foil open and sprinkle with parsley.

Serves 4.

SEA BASS IN PERNOD

4 4- to 6-ounce fillets of
   sea bass
  salt and freshly ground
   pepper
1 cup fish stock or
  bottled clam juice

1 large onion, thinly
   sliced
2 tablespoons pernod
2 teaspoons fresh
   chopped parsley

Season bass fillets with salt and pepper. Place fish stock or clam juice, onion and pernod in skillet and bring to a boil. Reduce heat, add fillets, cover and simmer for 12 minutes. Remove fillets to warmed serving dish, and cover to keep warm. Reduce liquid in skillet over high heat for 3 minutes. Strain and pour over fish. Sprinkle with parsley.

Serves 4.

SHRIMP AND MUSHROOMS

1 pound medium
   cooked shrimp
2 teaspoons butter
1 teaspoon vegetable
   oil
3 tablespoons dry
   sherry
½ pound thinly sliced
   mushrooms

¾ cup chicken stock
½ cup sour cream at
   room temperature
1 teaspoon fresh
   chopped parsley
salt and freshly ground
   pepper

Heat butter and oil with sherry in frying pan. Add
mushrooms and cook over medium heat for 5 minutes
stirring. Add chicken stock and bring to a boil, reduce
heat, and simmer for 5 minutes. Add shrimp and con
tinue simmering for 5 minutes. Remove from heat, stir in
sour cream and parsley, and season with salt and pepper

Serves 4.

TENDER SHRIMP IN TANGY TOMATO SAUCE

¾ pound shrimp,
  shelled and deveined
1½ cups water
1 cup dry vermouth
3 tablespoons lemon
  juice
1 teaspoon oil
1½ cups tomato sauce
1 onion, chopped fine
1 tablespoon
  Worcestershire
  sauce

1 tablespoon vinegar
2 drops Tabasco sauce
¼ cup finely chopped
  celery
½ teaspoon dried basil
½ teaspoon dried
  oregano
salt and freshly
  ground pepper to
  taste

Bring water and vermouth to a boil, and cook shrimp for 3 minutes. Drain and place shrimp in bowl with lemon juice and oil. Toss, cover, and set aside. In saucepan, add remaining ingredients and simmer for 30 minutes. Add shrimp and cook for 5 minutes. Serve in individual ramekins.

Serves 4.

STEAMED LOBSTER WITH *SAUCE VERTE*

4 1-pound lobsters
   water
½ teaspoon salt

¾ cup *sauce verte* (See index for recipe)

Cover bottom of lobster pot or other large pot with water, add salt, and bring to a boil. Add lobsters and steam for about 15 minutes. Remove from pot and drain. Split lobsters open lengthwise with large butcher knife, and remove intestine and sac. Place each lobster on large plate, and serve with *sauce verte* and lemon wedge.

Serves 4.

Poultry

Always thinning, now more so, poultry is the elegant way to keep a gourmet meal within *minceur* lines.

CHICKEN BREASTS *CLASSIQUE*

4 chicken breasts, boned and left whole
2 teaspoons butter
2 tablespoons finely chopped shallots
3 tablespoons fresh chopped parsley
¼ cup finely chopped watercress
½ teaspoon dried tarragon
3 tablespoons dry white wine
3 tablespoons dried bread crumbs
salt and freshly ground pepper to taste
¾ cup chicken stock

Melt butter in skillet. Sauté shallots for 3 minutes, stirring. Add parsley, watercress, tarragon, white wine, bread crumbs, and salt and pepper to taste. Stir and cook for 3 or 4 minutes over medium heat. Separate skin from each chicken breast and spread mixture over top of chicken breast meat. Place chicken skins back over top of breasts and fold ends of each breast under itself. Place in baking dish which is just large enough to comfortably hold chicken, and pour in broth. Cover dish with lid or foil and place in preheated 350° F. oven and bake for 20 minutes. Remove cover and bake 20 minutes more or until chicken is browned on top.

Serves 4.

CHICKEN NORMANDY STYLE

1 3½-pound chicken,
  cut into 8 serving
  pieces
  salt and freshly
  ground pepper
1 tablespoon butter
1 tablespoon vegetable
  oil
3 tablespoons Calvados
  or brandy

1 medium-large
  onion, chopped
1½ cups apple juice
2 cooking apples,
  peeled, cored, and
  sliced
½ pound mushrooms,
  sliced

Season chicken with salt and pepper. Heat butter and oil in large skillet, and brown chicken on both sides. Remove chicken, and pat off fat with absorbent paper. Wipe fat from pan, and add Calvados and onion. Cook over high heat for 2 minutes, stirring. Add apple juice and chicken and bring to a boil, reduce heat, cover and simmer for 15 minutes. Add apples, re-cover, and simmer for 10 minutes. Add mushrooms, cover and cook 5 minutes. Check seasoning.

Serves 4.

CHICKEN POACHED IN LEMON BROTH

1 3½-pound chicken
1 quart chicken stock
1 medium onion, halved
1 carrot, scraped and
   sliced into 1-inch
   lengths
1 stalk celery, chopped
1 bay leaf
¼ cup lemon juice
⅛ teaspoon freshly
   ground pepper

3 tablespoons *crème
   fraîche* (See index
   for recipe)
½ cup yogurt
1 tablespoon lemon
   juice
1 tablespoon fresh
   chopped parsley
salt and freshly ground
   pepper to taste

Truss chicken and place in pot with stock, onion, carrot, celery, bay leaf, lemon juice, and pepper. Bring to a boil, reduce heat, cover, and simmer for 1 hour. For the sauce, combine *crème fraîche*, yogurt, lemon juice, parsley, and salt and pepper in a small bowl. Leave sauce at room temperature. Remove chicken when done and let rest for 5 minutes. Carve off leg and thigh sections and place on heated serving dish. Carve breast and wing sections from chicken and arrange on dish. Strain liquid from pot until you have ½ cup of lemon broth and spoon over chicken. Serve sauce in gravy boat.

Serves 4.

CHICKEN SAUTÉ WITH CAPERS

8 serving pieces chicken
2 tablespoons vegetable
   oil
½ cup dry white wine
1 medium onion, sliced
1 clove garlic, minced
2 medium-large
   tomatoes, peeled,
   seeded, and chopped

salt and freshly ground
   pepper to taste
¼ teaspoon dried
   oregano
1 cup chicken stock
2 tablespoons capers

Season chicken with salt and pepper. Heat oil in
skillet and brown chicken on all sides over medium
high heat. Remove chicken from pan and with absorbent
paper pat off as much oil as possible. Clean skillet. Add
3 tablespoons wine to skillet, and bring to a boil. Add
onion, garlic, and tomatoes, and cook until most of
moisture has evaporated. Season with salt and pepper and
oregano. Return chicken to pan. Pour in rest of wine and
stock. Sprinkle capers over chicken. Bring to a boil, reduce heat to a simmer, cover, and cook for 25 minutes.

Serves 4.

CHICKEN *TANDOORI*

1 3½-pound chicken, quartered, back and breastbone removed
1 cup plain yogurt
2 cloves garlic, crushed
1 teaspoon cumin
1 teaspoon turmeric
1 teaspoon ginger
½ teaspoon cinnamon
2 teaspoons coriander

3 tablespoons grated onion
pinch of cayenne pepper
¼ cup fresh lime juice
salt and freshly ground pepper to taste
4 teaspoons melted butter
4 slices fresh lime

In bowl combine yogurt, garlic, cumin, turmeric, ginger, cinnamon, coriander, onion, cayenne pepper, lime juice, salt and pepper. Prick chicken quarters with fork in several places, and turn each piece in mixture until well coated. Cover and marinate in refrigerator overnight. Turn chicken pieces once during marination. Place chicken on lightly greased shallow baking dish, skin side up. Sprinkle 1 teaspoon of melted butter over each. Bake in preheated 375° F. oven for about 45 minutes, or until tender.

Garnish each serving with 1 slice of fresh lime.

Serves 4.

8 serving pieces
  chicken
  salt and freshly
    ground pepper
2 tablespoons butter
2 tablespoons chopped
  shallots
1 large clove garlic,
  crushed
1½ cups dry red
  Burgundy
1 cup beef stock
1 bay leaf
1 teaspoon finely
  chopped parsley
1 tablespoon tomato
  paste

¼ teaspoon thyme
  salt and pepper to
    taste
2 tablespoons Cognac
½ cup onion purée (See
  index for recipe)
1 tablespoon butter
2 tablespoons red
  Burgundy
½ pound sliced
  mushrooms
2 ripe tomatoes, peeled
  and cut into wedges
  fresh chopped parsley

Season chicken with salt and pepper. In large skillet heat 2 tablespoons butter and brown chicken on each side. Remove chicken and pat free of as much fat as possible with absorbent paper. Add shallots and garlic and cook over low heat for 1 minute. Return chicken to pan. Add red wine, beef stock, bay leaf, parsley, tomato paste, thyme, salt and pepper to taste. Bring to a boil, reduce heat, cover, and simmer for 25 minutes. Remove chicken, strain liquid in pan, and put it in saucepan. Add Cognac and puréed onions. Cook over medium-high heat for 5 minutes, stirring. Melt 1 tablespoon butter in clean skillet, add 2 tablespoons Burgundy, and bring to a boil. Add mushrooms and cook over medium heat for minutes, stirring occasionally. Return chicken to large skillet with sauce, mushrooms, and tomatoes. Cook for 2 or 3 minutes. Check seasoning.

Serves 4.

CRISP OVEN CHICKEN

2 chicken breasts, halved, breastbone removed	1 tablespoon chopped onion
4 thighs	½ teaspoon seasoned salt
3 tablespoons vegetable oil	¼ teaspoon minced garlic
2 tablespoons lemon juice	½ teaspoon paprika freshly ground pepper to taste

Place vegetable oil, lemon, and onion in blender and purée. Add remaining ingredients and combine well. Brush each piece of chicken on both sides with mixture. Place chicken on baking sheet, skin side up. Bake in preheated 350° F. oven for 45 minutes.

Serves 4.

CURRIED CHICKEN WITH PEACHES

1 3½-pound chicken, cut into 8 serving pieces

salt and freshly ground pepper

2 tablespoons vegetable oil

1 medium onion, thinly sliced

2 cloves garlic, crushed

1 tablespoon curry powder

1 cup chicken stock

3 fresh ripe peaches, peeled, pitted, and sliced

½ cup plain yogurt

Season chicken with salt and pepper. Heat oil in skillet, and brown chicken. Remove chicken to side dish. Add onion and garlic. Sauté for 3 minutes, stirring frequently. Sprinkle onions with curry powder and return chicken to pan. Add stock and bring to a boil. Reduce heat, cover, and simmer for 25 minutes. Remove chicken from pan to heated serving dish. Reduce liquid in pan over high heat for 3 minutes. Add peach slices and cook for 1 minute. Remove pan from heat and stir in yogurt. Check seasoning. Spoon sauce and peaches over chicken.

Serves 4.

MADEIRAN CHICKEN

1 3½-pound roasting
   chicken
salt and freshly ground
   pepper
1 tablespoon butter
1 large red or green
   pepper, cleaned and
   cut into thin strips

1 large yellow onion, cut
   into slivers
1 cup Madeira

Truss chicken and season well all over with salt and pepper. Heat butter in 10-inch skillet and rub over bottom of pan. Over medium-high heat brown only breast of chicken. Place pepper strips and sliced onions in casserole just large enough to hold chicken. Place chicken over peppers and onions. Pour in Madeira. Season chicken with salt and pepper, cover, and place in preheated 375° F. oven for 1 hour. Remove chicken and let rest for 15 minutes. Cut into individual pieces, or quarter. Place in serving dish and surround with peppers, onions, and Madeira broth.

Serves 4.

MARINATED BROILED CHICKEN

8 serving pieces chicken
juice of two lemons
1 tablespoon vegetable
oil
1 tablespoon grated
onion
1 clove garlic, crushed

½ teaspoon curry
powder
½ teaspoon cumin
2 tablespoons dry sherry
⅛ teaspoon salt
freshly ground pepper
to taste

Combine all ingredients but chicken in bowl large enough to hold chicken. With pointed knife prick each piece of chicken in several places on each side. Place chicken in marinade and turn so that each piece is evenly coated. Cover bowl and refrigerate overnight, or at least 8 hours. Turn once during marination. Broil chicken on roasting rack 3 or 4 inches from heat until crisp on each side.

Serves 4.

POULET IRENE

4 small chicken breasts, boned and halved
salt and freshly ground pepper
1 teaspoon butter
1 tablespoon vegetable oil
1 leek, white part only, chopped fine
½ teaspoon rosemary
½ teaspoon marjoram
¼ pound mushrooms
½ cup dry white wine
½ cup chicken stock
2 tomatoes, peeled and cut into wedges
2 tablespoons brandy

Season chicken with salt and pepper. Heat butter with oil in large skillet. Brown breasts on skin sides only, then remove to side dish. Add leek and stir over low heat for 1 minute. Return chicken to pan, breasts sides down, with all ingredients except tomatoes and brandy. Bring to a boil, reduce heat, cover, and simmer for 20 minutes. Add tomatoes, re-cover, and cook for 3 minutes. Stir in brandy and bring to a boil.

Garnish with fresh chopped parsley.

Serves 4.

POACHED CHICKEN WITH SEAFOOD
AND VEGETABLES
(Cover photo)

An important aspect of slimming cooking is to keep a dish from being too bland to satisfy the palate. This dish, created one snowy night, especially cheered me because of the variety of protein and flavorful vegetables which proved as attractive to the eye as to the tastebuds. The dish does require several procedures and extra preparation time, and should be approached with attention and care.

1 3½-pound whole chicken
1 quart chicken stock
2 cups water
1 medium onion, halved
1 bouquet garni
½ cup dry vermouth
1 pound mussels
½ pound medium shrimp

1 10-ounce package frozen artichoke hearts
16 asparagus spears
2 carrots, scraped and shaped into 1½-by-¾-inch barrels
salt and freshly ground pepper to taste

Sauce:

2 tablespoons butter
1½ tablespoons flour
1¾ cup hot fish stock or chicken stock
2 tablespoons Cognac
salt and pepper to taste

3 tablespoons *crème fraîche* (See index for recipe)
1½ tablespoons freshly chopped parsley

In a 4-quart ovenproof casserole, large enough to hold chicken, place chicken stock and water with onion and bouquet garni. Bring to a boil. Gently lower trussed chicken into liquid and reduce heat to a simmer. Cover and cook for 45 minutes. Turn off heat and let chicken rest in liquid for 30 minutes. Meanwhile, clean mussels and steam them in ¼ cup dry vermouth and ½ cup water for 8 minutes. Drain and remove empty half shells. Set aside. Next, cook shrimp in 2 cups lightly salted boiling water with ¼ cup dry vermouth for 4 minutes. Drain and remove shells when cool enough to handle, leaving tails intact. Set aside. In separate saucepans, cook vegetables in lightly salted water, simmering, until vegetables are tender. Drain. Place vegetables in vegetable steamer over hot water to keep warm.

In clean small suacepan melt butter and stir in flour and cook for 2 or 3 minutes, stirring constantly with whisk. Pour in fish or chicken stock and stir with whisk until sauce comes to a boil and has thickened slightly. Season with salt and pepper. Add *crème fraîche* and Cognac, and stir over high heat for 1 minute. Check seasoning and remove from heat. Stir in parsley. Cover.

Remove chicken from pot and carve off leg and thigh joints. Then carve off side of breast and wing. Return chicken pieces to strained hot liquid they cooked in. Bring 1 cup water to a boil and place shrimp in water for 30 seconds. Remove from heat and strain water off mussels in colander. Spoon sauce evenly over bottom of four warmed dinner plates. Place ¼ of chicken in the center of each plate over sauce. Arrange seafood and vegetables around plates in equal proportions. Spoon a little sauce over chicken and mussels.

Serves 4.

ROAST CHICKEN WITH DILL SAUCE

1 3½-pound roasting
   chicken
1 small onion, halved
3 or 4 full sprigs fresh
   dill or 1 teaspoon
   dried dillweed
2 teaspoons butter,
   softened
  salt and freshly ground
   pepper

½ cup dry white wine
1 cup chicken broth
1 teaspoon cornstarch
1 teaspoon fresh
   chopped dill or
   ½ teaspoon dried
   dillweed
1 tablespoon butter
   (optional)

Put onion and sprig of dill inside chicken and truss. Rub surface of chicken with 2 teaspoons softened butter, and sprinkle with salt and pepper. Place in small roasting pan. Add wine and broth. Put in preheated 350° F. oven and cook for 1½ hours, or until tender. Baste with liquid in pan every 15 minutes. Transfer chicken from pan to warmed platter and strain juices. Put liquid in pan and bring to a boil. Mix cornstarch with 1 tablespoon water and dissolve cornstarch by stirring. Whisk mixture into sauce and add dill. Check seasoning and swirl in 1 tablespoon butter, if desired.

Carve chicken, or quarter, and serve with sauce.

Serves 4.

ROAST CAPON WITH MUSHROOMS
AND ONIONS

1 6-pound capon salt and freshly ground pepper	1 cup chopped onions ½ pound mushrooms, quartered
2 teaspoons butter	½ cup chicken stock
1 tablespoon butter	½ teaspoon dried
2 tablespoons dry white wine	tarragon ¼ cup *crème fraîche*

Season inside cavity of capon and outside with salt and pepper, and truss. Place capon on large sheet of heavy-duty aluminum foil. Brush capon with 1 teaspoon of melted butter, and fold foil around bird securely. Place in roasting pan in preheated 400° F. oven for 1 hour. Remove foil from around capon and brush with 1 teaspoon butter. Reduce heat to 375° F. and cook for about 15 minutes more, or until capon has browned and is tender. Let rest 15 minutes before carving. Meanwhile, heat 1 tablespoon butter in large skillet with wine. Add onions and cook for 5 minutes, stirring. Add mushrooms, stir, cover, and cook for 5 minutes over medium-low heat. Add chicken stock and tarragon, and cook over high heat for 5 minutes. Remove from heat, stir in *crème fraîche*. Carve capon and serve with mushrooms and onions.

Serves 6.

CORNISH GAME HENS BAKED
IN SOY SAUCE

4 Cornish game hens
  salt and pepper
2 medium onions,
  peeled and halved
½ cup soy sauce

½ cup orange juice
1 cup chicken stock
1 clove garlic, crushed
2 teaspoons oil

Season inside cavity of hens and sprinkle skin with salt and pepper. Place half an onion in cavity of each bird, and truss. Combine soy sauce, orange juice, chicken stock, and garlic. Place hens in baking dish and pour soy sauce mixture into dish. Cover with foil and place in preheated 375° F. oven and cook for 30 minutes. Remove foil and brush birds with oil. Bake for 15 minutes, or until tender and brown.

Serves 4.

BRAISED DUCK

1 4½-pound duck
  salt and freshly ground
  pepper
1 medium onion,
  chopped
2 carrots, scraped and
  sliced

1 clove garlic, minced
½ teaspoon dried sage,
  crumbled
¼ teaspoon dried thyme
2 cups dry white wine
4 cups beef stock

Salt and pepper inside cavity and skin of duck. Prick skin around thigh area to release as much fat as possible. Place duck in shallow baking dish under broiler about 3 inches from heat. Cook for about 15 minutes, turning often, browning all sides. Remove. Place duck in casserole with remaining ingredients. Bring to a boil. Cover and place in preheated 350° F. oven and cook for 1½ hours. While cooking, turn duck twice. Remove duck when cooked, and let rest for 5 minutes. Meanwhile, strain liquid and reserve vegetables. Skim off as much fat as possible from liquid. Heat liquid in saucepan and reduce to half over high heat. Purée vegetables in blender and whisk into sauce. Quarter duck and serve with sauce.

Serves 4.

Beef, Lamb, and Veal

Cuisine minceur meat should always be selected for leanness of cut and trimmed of any fat. Pork is rarely used, as it is too fattening. So, I have tried to select recipes that are particularly suited to this method and are also interesting to serve.

AMERICAN POT ROAST *MINCEUR*

1 3-pound lean boneless chuck roast	2 carrots, scraped and quartered
2 tablespoons vegetable oil	1 bay leaf
salt and freshly ground pepper	1 16-ounce can whole tomatoes and liquid
3 tablespoons red wine	½ cup tomato paste
2 medium onions, peeled and left whole	1½ cups dry red wine
1 large clove garlic, chopped	1½ cups beef stock
	¼ teaspoon dried thyme
	¼ teaspoon freshly ground pepper
	½ teaspoon paprika
	¼ teaspoon salt

In 4- or 5-quart heavy casserole or Dutch oven heat oil. Season roast with salt and pepper. Over high heat, brown roast on top and bottom. Remove roast and pat meat free of as much fat as possible. Add 3 tablespoons red wine, onions, garlic, and carrots. Stir and cook over medium heat for 1 minute. Place roast on top of vegetables, and add remaining ingredients. Bring to a boil. Cover casserole, and place in preheated 325° F. oven for 1½ hours. Turn roast, re-cover, and cook for 1 hour longer, or until meat is tender. Remove roast and cover to keep warm. Discard bay leaf. Spoon off as much fat as possible on surface of liquid the roast cooked in, and strain. Purée vegetables in food processor or force through food mill and reserve. Bring liquid in saucepan to a boil and cook for 10 minutes. Spoon off fat that rises to surface. Whisk puréed vegetables into liquid. Check seasoning for taste. Cook, stirring, for about 5 minutes. Carve roast and serve with sauce.

Serves 4 to 6.

BEEF *BOURGUIGNONNE*

2 pounds lean rump of
  beef, cut into
  1½-inch cubes
salt and freshly ground
  pepper
1 tablespoon vegetable
  oil
2 teaspoons butter
1 large clove garlic,
  minced
1 tablespoon finely
  chopped shallots
1 medium-large onion,
  chopped

2 carrots, scraped and
  sliced
¼ cup Cognac, warmed
1 bay leaf
½ teaspoon dried thyme
½ bottle red Burgundy
  water
18 small white onions,
  peeled and left whole
2 cups chicken stock
½ pound mushrooms
1 teaspoon lemon juice

Sprinkle meat with salt and pepper. Heat oil and
butter in heavy 3-quart Dutch oven or pot. Brown meat
on all sides over medium-high heat. Remove meat, and
remove as much fat as possible by patting with absorbent
paper. Wipe pot free of fat. Add garlic, shallots, onions,
and carrots. Pour warmed Cognac in pan. Ignite Cognac.
When flame goes out, return meat, add bay leaf, thyme,
Burgundy, and enough water to cover meat. Cover and
cook over low heat about 1½ hours until meat is
tender. Half an hour before beef is tender, bring stock to
a boil in saucepan. Add onions and simmer for 20 minutes until tender. In another saucepan heat 2 cups of
water with lemon juice and salt and pepper. Simmer
mushrooms for 5 minutes. Remove meat from pot to side

dish. Discard bay leaf. Strain sauce. Purée carrots and add to sauce in clean pot with meat, drained onions, and mushrooms. Check seasoning and heat through.

Serves 6.

BOILED BEEF

1 3-pound lean brisket of beef
3 leeks, trimmed, washed well, and halved
1 carrot, scraped and quartered
1 stalk celery, chopped
1 bay leaf
½ teaspoon dried thyme
10 peppercorns

Bring to boil enough water to cover meat in a heavy Dutch oven or large pot. Add all ingredients, cover, and simmer for about 3 hours, until meat is tender.

Slice and serve with horseradish sauce (See index for recipe) and fresh cooked vegetables.

Serves 6.

GROUND BEEF *AU POIVRE* WITH
BÉARNAISE SAUCE *MINCEUR*

1 ⅓ pounds lean ground beef

2 teaspoons Worcestershire sauce

1 tablespoon grated onion

¼ teaspoon salt

2 teaspoons freshly ground pepper

4 rounded tablespoons béarnaise sauce *minceur* (See index for recipe)

Combine ground beef, Worcestershire sauce, onion, and salt. Shape into 4 hamburgers. Sprinkle pepper on each side of burgers and press into meat. Sprinkle 1 teaspoon salt over bottom of frying pan and heat until salt begins to turn color. Sauté burgers until brown on one side, turn, and cook to desired doneness. Top each with rounded tablespoon of béarnaise sauce *minceur*.

Serves 4.

MEATLOAF *MINCEUR*

1 pound lean ground
  beef
1 small onion, grated
3 tablespoons minced
  green pepper
1 egg white
1 tablespoon soy sauce
¼ teaspoon dried
  oregano
¼ teaspoon dried
  tarragon

1 tablespoon dry red
  wine
¼ teaspoon salt
  freshly ground pepper
  to taste
½ cup tomato sauce
  minceur (See index
  for recipe

In large bowl combine ground beef, onion, green
pepper, egg white, soy sauce, oregano, tarragon, red wine,
salt, and pepper. Shape into loaf and place in lightly
greased loaf pan. Bake in preheated 375° F. oven for
½ hour. Pour tomato sauce *minceur* over meatloaf, and
cook for 30 minutes more.

Serves 4.

ROAST BEEF AND CUCUMBERS IN HORSERADISH SAUCE

½ pound sliced lean
   roast beef, cut into
   thin strips
1 medium cucumber,
   peeled

½ cup horseradish sauce
   (See index for
   recipe)
½ pound fresh spinach,
   rinsed, patted dry

Cut cucumber in half lengthwise. Scoop out seeds with spoon. Thinly slice cucumber and combine with roast beef strips. Add horseradish sauce and toss.

Serve on bed of raw chopped spinach.

Serves 4.

SAUERBRATEN

1 3½-to-4-pound
    lean rump roast
    salt and freshly
    ground pepper
2 cups red wine
    vinegar
2 cups water
½ tablespoons sugar

1 medium onion,
    halved
1 large clove garlic,
    minced
2 cloves
1 bay leaf, crumbled
6 peppercorns
½ cup sour cream

Season meat well with salt and pepper, and place in large bowl. In saucepan bring vinegar and water to a boil. Add onion and remaining ingredients, except sour cream. Pour over beef, cover, and cool. Refrigerate overnight. Place marinade and beef in heavy pot or Dutch oven and bring to a boil. Reduce heat, cover, and simmer for about 3 hours, until meat is tender. Remove meat and cover to keep warm. Strain liquid in pot and return to saucepan. Reduce liquid over high heat for minutes. Stir in ½ cup of sour cream and serve with sliced meat.

Serves 8.

TOURNEDOS OF BEEF WITH PURÉED ONION

4 1¼-inch-thick fillets   puréed onions (See
   of beef   index for recipe)
1 teaspoon salt

Sprinkle salt on bottom of heavy skillet and heat un
salt begins to turn in color. Add steaks and cook ov
high heat until browned. Turn and cook to desired don
ness.

Serve with puréed onions.

Serves 4.

STUFFED FLANK STEAK

1 2½-pound flank steak, trimmed of as much fat as possible
salt and freshly ground pepper
1 teaspoon minced garlic
2 carrots, scraped and sliced into thin strips lengthwise
2 onions, cut into thin rings
¼ pound fresh chopped spinach
2 tablespoons vegetable oil
1 carrot, scraped and chopped
1 stalk celery, chopped
1 bay leaf
1 cup red wine
2 cups beef stock

Butterfly steak by cutting through center of meat's thickness lengthwise until you are about ½ inch from opposite side of opening. Spread open and sprinkle meat with salt, pepper, and garlic. Arrange carrots across steak. Top with onion rings and spinach. Roll up steak and tie with string. Heat oil in Dutch oven or large pot. Brown meat quickly over high heat on all sides. Remove and pat off as much fat from meat as possible. Wipe out fat from pan with absorbent paper. Add remaining ingredients and bring to a boil. Replace meat and bring to a boil again. Cover and place in preheated 350° F. oven for 1½ hours, turning meat twice during cooking time. Remove meat and let rest on carving board. Meanwhile, remove bay leaf and discard. Strain liquid from pot and return to saucepan. Over high heat reduce liquid for 3 minutes. Purée vegetables and return to liquid. Check seasoning.

Slice meat and serve with sauce.

Serves 4 to 6.

BONED LAMB CHOPS IN WINE SAUCE

4 1-inch-thick boned
   lamb chops (4 to 6
   ounces each)
   salt
½ cup dry white wine
1 tablespoon finely
   chopped shallots

½ cup chicken stock
½ teaspoon dried thyme
3 tablespoons *crème
   fraîche* (See index
   for recipe)
1 teaspoon finely
   chopped parsley

Tie each lamb chop with string to hold together. Sprinkle about ½ teaspoon salt over bottom of heavy skillet, and heat until salt begins to turn golden. Over medium-high heat brown rolled chops on each side. Transfer lamb to side dish and clean skillet. Heat tablespoons wine. Add shallots and cook for 3 minutes. Add remaining wine and other ingredients, except *crème fraîche* and parsley, and bring to a boil, reduce heat, cover, and cook for 20 minutes. Remove lamb and reduce liquid over high heat for 3 minutes. Remove pan from heat and stir in *crème fraîche* and pour over lamb. Sprinkle with parsley.

Serves 4.

BRAISED LAMB SHOULDER

4 lean shoulder lamb
   chops, trimmed of as
   much fat as possible
salt and freshly ground
   pepper
2 teaspoons butter
1 teaspoon oil
1 clove garlic,
   minced

3 tablespoons soy sauce
2 tablespoons dry sherry
¾ cup chicken stock
1 leek, white part only,
   well washed and
   chopped

Season chops with salt and pepper. In large skillet, heat butter with oil. Brown chops on each side. Remove to side dish. Add garlic and cook, stirring, for ½ minute. Return meat to pan with soy sauce, sherry, and stock. Bring to a boil, reduce heat, and simmer, covered, for 15 minutes. Add leek, re-cover, and simmer for 15 minutes.

Serves 4.

LAMB CURRY WITH VEGETABLES

1 pound lean boneless
    lamb, cut into 1-inch
      cubes
2 teaspoons butter
1 teaspoon vegetable
    oil
1 clove garlic, crushed
1 medium onion,
    chopped
salt and freshly ground
    pepper
¼ teaspoon cinnamon

½ teaspoon cardamom
1 teaspoon ginger
1 teaspoon coriander
½ teaspoon turmeric
1 cup plain yogurt
½ pound cooked sliced
    carrots
½ pound cooked
    asparagus cut into
    1-inch lengths
1 boiled potato, peeled
    and diced

Heat butter and vegetable oil in skillet. Sauté garlic and onion for 3 minutes, stirring often. Remove garlic and onion. Add lamb, seasoned with salt and pepper, and brown on all sides. Return onions and garlic with remaining ingredients and stir. Simmer for about 30 minutes, covered. Add well-drained cooked vegetables, and heat through over low heat. Add a little chicken stock if too thick.

Serves 4.

LAMB KEBABS

2 pounds boned leg of
  lamb, cut into
  1½-inch cubes, all
  fat removed from
  meat
1 cup plain yogurt
1 small onion, grated
1 clove garlic, crushed
2 tablespoons lemon
  juice

1 teaspoon cumin
½ teaspoon cinnamon
½ teaspoon ginger
½ teaspoon coriander
½ teaspoon salt
  freshly ground pepper
  to taste
1 cup 1-inch slices of
  onion

In bowl combine all ingredients except lamb and cup of onion slices. Add lamb and turn until well coated with mixture. Cover and refrigerate for 8 hours or overnight. Thread lamb cubes on skewers between slices of onion. Place skewers on broiler rack and broil about 18 minutes of total cooking time. Turn skewers so meat is evenly cooked and browned.

Serves 6.

MARINATED LAMB CHOPS

4 1-inch-thick lean lamb chops
½ cup soy sauce
1 clove garlic, crushed

1 scallion, minced
3 tablespoons orange juice

Combine soy sauce, garlic, scallions, and orange juice in bowl. In shallow dish place lamb chops, pour marinade over chops, and cover. Refrigerate for 8 hours or overnight. On broiler rack cook 3 inches from heated broiler for 8 minutes. Turn and brush with marinade. Cook 6 minutes longer or until desired doneness reached.

Serves 4.

NAVARIN OF LAMB

2 pounds lean lamb
   shoulder, cut into
   1½-inch cubes
salt and freshly ground
   pepper
1 clove garlic, crushed
1 bay leaf, crumbled

¼ teaspoon dried thyme
2 ripe tomatoes, peeled,
   seeded, and chopped
1 cup cooked green peas
4 sliced cooked carrots
8 cooked small white
   onions

Season lamb with salt and pepper. Heat oil and brown meat. Remove meat and pat dry on all sides with absorbent paper. Return meat to pan with stock, garlic, bay leaf, thyme, and chopped tomatoes. Bring to a boil, reduce heat, and simmer for about 1½ hours, until meat is tender. Transfer meat to saucepan. Spoon off as much fat from sauce as possible and return to meat with cooked vegetables. Combine gently. Check seasoning. When vegetables are heated through, dish is done. Garnish with fresh chopped parsley.

Serves 4.

HERBED VEAL CHOPS WITH GARLIC

4 1-inch-thick veal
  chops
  salt and freshly ground
  pepper
2 teaspoons butter
1 teaspoon oil
2 tablespoons dry white
  wine
2 tablespoons finely
  chopped shallots

2 large cloves garlic,
  crushed
½ cup chicken stock
¼ teaspoon rosemary
½ teaspoon tarragon
1 teaspoon fresh
  chopped parsley

Heat butter in skillet with oil. Season chops with salt and pepper. Brown chops on both sides. Remove from pan. Pat chops dry and wipe pan free of grease. Add wine, shallots, and garlic, and cook for 3 minutes. Add chicken stock and herbs. Pour into shallow baking dish large enough to comfortably hold chops. Place in preheated 350° F. oven and bake for 20 minutes. Turn chops and cook for another 20 minutes, or until tender.

Serves 4.

4 large thin veal scallops
  salt and freshly ground
  pepper
1 large clove garlic,
  minced
½ cup finely chopped
  onion
½ cup finely chopped
  fennel or celery
½ teaspoon dried
  oregano

½ teaspoon dried
  rosemary
2 tablespoons finely
  chopped parsley
2 teaspoons butter
1 teaspoon vegetable
  oil
½ cup dry white wine
½ cup chicken stock

Season veal with salt and pepper. Combine garlic, onion, fennel, oregano, rosemary, and parsley. Spread over scallops and roll up. Secure with string. Heat butter with oil in skillet and brown over medium-high heat on all sides. Pat veal birds dry in absorbent paper. Place in small shallow baking dish just large enough to hold birds and liquid. Add wine and chicken stock, cover, and bake in preheated 375° F. oven for 20 minutes. Remove cover and cook for about 15 minutes until veal is tender.

Serves 4.

VEAL RAGOUT

2 pounds veal, cut into
  1½-inch cubes
2 tablespoons vegetable
  oil
  salt and freshly
  ground pepper to
  taste
2 tablespoons finely
  chopped shallots

1½ cups chicken stock
1 cup dry white wine
2 teaspoons dried
  tarragon
3 tablespoons *crème
  fraîche* (See index
  for recipe)
  fresh chopped parsley

Heat oil in skillet. Season veal cubes with salt and pepper. Brown veal over high heat on all sides. Add shallots and stir. Cook for 2 minutes. Add stock, wine, and tarragon. Bring to a boil, reduce heat, and simmer for 1½ hours, or until veal is tender. Remove veal with slotted spoon. Over high heat reduce liquid to about 1½ cups. Return veal to sauce and remove from heat. Stir in *crème fraîche*. Sprinkle with parsley.

Serves 4.

Almost *Minceur*

For those days when some amount of starch seems irresistible or inevitable.

GREEN NOODLES IN SAVORY TOMATO SAUCE

1 tablespoon vegetable oil	¼ teaspoon dried oregano
1 tablespoon dry red wine	¼ teaspoon dried basil
1 medium onion, cut into 1-inch slivers	¼ teaspoon seasoned salt
1 large clove garlic, minced	¼ teaspoon salt
	freshly ground pepper
1 14½-ounce can whole tomatoes	8 ounces green noodles
	3 ounces skim-milk mozzarella cheese, cut into ¼-inch dice
1 8-ounce can tomato sauce	2 tablespoons vegetable oil

Heat 1 tablespoon oil and red wine in saucepan. Add onion and garlic. Cook for 4 minutes, stirring occasionally. Chop up tomatoes, removing stem ends (usually tough), and add with juice from can along with tomato sauce, oregano, basil, seasoned salt, salt, and pepper. Bring to a boil, reduce to a simmer, and cook for 20 minutes, stirring frequently. Continue to cook sauce over very low heat while cooking noodles. Bring 3½ quarts of lightly salted water to a boil in large pot. When water is rapidly boiling add noodles and cook over high heat until noodles are just tender, about 7 minutes. The only way to test actual doneness is to take a noodle out and taste it. Drain noodles well quickly and immediately pour sauce over noodles in large bowl. Gently toss so noodles are completely coated. Turn into lightly greased casserole dish and sprinkle with mozzarella and 2 tablespoons oil. Bake in preheated 400° F. oven until cheese is golden on top.

Serves 4 to 6.

PURÉE OF BAKED POTATO WITH ZUCCHINI

4 Idaho baking potatoes
1 medium-large
   zucchini, peeled
   and sliced
½ teaspoon seasoned
   salt

salt and freshly ground
   pepper to taste
½ cup skim milk, or as
   needed

Bake potatoes at 425° F. for 20 minutes. Pierce skin with fork and continue cooking until done. Minutes before potatoes are finished, place zucchini slices in saucepan with lightly salted water to cover. Cook for 8 minutes. Drain and set aside. When potatoes are cooked, cut ⅓ off the top of each potato lengthwise. With a spoon remove the pulp from the rest of the potatoes. Be sure not to break the skin on the shell. Place pulp in food processor with zucchini (or force through food mill). Add seasoning and milk, and process or mix until smooth. Add more milk if necessary to make mixture fluffy. Adjust seasoning. Spoon equal amounts of mixture into potato shells and place on baking sheet under broiler until tops are golden.

Serves 4.

SPAGHETTI *MINCEUR*

8 ounces thin spaghetti
2 teaspoons vegetable
  oil
2 medium zucchini,
  diced
salt
2 cups tomato sauce
  minceur (See index
  for recipe)

3 tablespoons freshly
  grated Parmesan
  cheese
freshly ground pepper

Cook spaghetti according to package directions in rolling boiling water with vegetable oil. Meanwhile bring 2 cups of water to a boil in saucepan. Add a little salt. Cook zucchini in water for 6 minutes. Drain and add to tomato sauce *minceur*. Heat. Drain cooked spaghetti and place in serving bowl. Top with sauce and zucchini mixture and sprinkle with Parmesan cheese and several grinds of pepper. Toss.

Serves 4 as appetizer or side dish.

Chinese Cuisine *Minceur*

Chinese cooking falls naturally into any *cuisine minceur* collection because little fat is used and ingredients are usually cooked quickly. Steaming and braising, which are important in Chinese cooking, are excellent *minceur* cooking methods. And even stir-fried food uses little enough fat to be acceptable. I have included several Chinese recipes to illustrate this. The only recipe in the book containing pork is a stir-fry recipe that uses only ½ pound of lean pork with vegetables.

CHINESE MIXED VEGETABLE SOUP

1 quart chicken broth, all fat removed
1 bean curd, cubed
6 mushrooms, thinly sliced
6 ounces snow pea pods
6 water chestnuts, thinly sliced

¼ pound fresh spinach leaves, chopped fine
1 scallion, minced
1 tablespoon soy sauce
1 tablespoon dry sherry

Bring chicken broth to a boil. Add remaining ingredients and bring to a boil again, reduce heat, and simmer for 3 minutes.

Serves 4 to 6.

STEAMED POMPANO CHINESE-STYLE

2 1-pound pompano
1 tablespoon dry sherry
1 tablespoon light soy
  sauce
1 tablespoon peanut or
  vegetable oil

2 scallions, cut into thin
  slivers
1 teaspoon shredded
  ginger root

Brush each side of fish with combined sherry and soy sauce. Place on shallow ovenproof platter. Cover fish with ginger root and scallions. Place on rack over boiling water in steamer, cover, and steam for about 20 minutes.

Serves 3 to 4.

CHINESE-STYLE PORK WITH VEGETABLES

½ pound lean boneless pork, cut into thin strips (easier to accomplish if meat is frozen)
1 teaspoon cornstarch
1 tablespoon egg white
1 tablespoon peanut or vegetable oil
1 tablespoon dry sherry
1 tablespoon soy sauce

1 green pepper, cored, seeded, and cut into thin strips 1 inch long
4 mushrooms, thinly sliced
2 ripe tomatoes, peeled and cut into wedges
1 scallion, chopped
¾ cup chicken stock
salt and pepper to taste
1 tablespoon cornstarch

Sprinkle 1 teaspoon cornstarch over pork and mix. Add egg white and mix, cover, and refrigerate for 30 minutes. Heat oil in skillet, add garlic and pork, and stir-fry for 3 minutes. Add sherry and soy sauce, and cook, stirring, for 1 minute. Add vegetables, cover, and cook for 2 minutes. Stir and add broth and season with salt and pepper. Cover and cook for 2 more minutes. Add final cornstarch which has been dissolved in a little water. Stir until sauce thickens slightly.

Serves 4.

STIR-FRIED CHINESE VEGETABLES

2 tablespoons peanut or vegetable oil

2 slices fresh ginger root

1 clove garlic, minced

4 trimmed asparagus stalks, cut on the diagonal into 1-inch lengths

3 stalks broccoli, trimmed and cut into bite-sized pieces

1 cup cauliflower in small flowerets

6 mushrooms, thinly sliced

¼ cup thinly sliced water chestnuts

2 tablespoons soy sauce

½ cup chicken stock

1 dozen snow peas, ends trimmed and threads removed

½ teaspoon sesame oil salt to taste

Heat oil in wok or skillet. Add ginger root and garlic. Stir-fry over high heat for 15 seconds. Add vegetables except for snow pea pods for 30 seconds over medium heat. Add soy sauce and stock. Stir-fry for 30 seconds until both come to a boil. Cover and cook for 4 or 5 minutes until vegetables are just tender crisp. Stir in snow pea pods and sesame oil, and season with salt.

Serves 4.

STIR-FRIED SOLE WITH BROCCOLI

½ pound fillets of sole, cut into 1-inch-by-½-inch pieces
1 teaspoon cornstarch
2 teaspoons light soy sauce
2 tablespoons peanut or vegetable oil
1 teaspoon shredded ginger root

5 broccoli spears, cut into 1½-by-½-inch lengths
½ cup chicken stock
salt
2 teaspoons cornstarch
2 tablespoons water
1 teaspoon sesame oil

Sprinkle fish pieces with cornstarch and add soy sauce. Heat oil in wok or skillet and gently stir-fry fish with ginger until fish turns white. Transfer fish to side dish. Add broccoli and stock, cover, and cook for 4 minutes until tender crisp. Return fish to wok, and season with salt. Add cornstarch which has been mixed with water and sesame oil. Gently turn until sauce thickens slightly.

Serves 4.

ALMOND FLOAT

Almond float or jelly is a lovely Chinese sweet dish from the province of Canton. It is traditionally served with fresh or canned fruit such as melon, pineapple, or mandarin oranges or lichees. The float is sliced into shapes such as diamonds, circles, or squares and surrounded with sectioned fruit. Converting almond float to *cuisine minceur* was done by substituting skim milk for milk.

1 envelope unflavored gelatin

½ cup cold water

3 tablespoons sugar

1½ cups skim milk at room temperature

¾ teaspoon almond extract

Soften gelatin in cold water. Add sugar and heat, stirring, until gelatin dissolves. Remove from heat and slowly stir in skim milk. Add almond extract and stir. Pour into shallow bowl. Chill until set.

Serves 6.

Desserts

A meal without dessert is an unfinished symphony. But how to remain true to the new cuisine and still have dessert? Fruit is the answer, of course. Fresh, naturally sweet, ripe fruit is always a treat—strawberries with a few dollops of *crème fraîche* is classic—but there are other ways of preparing fruit that make it even more elegant and special. I have tried to include a large number here.

For an unusual touch to accompany your fruit dessert see the almond float recipe in the Chinese *cuisine minceur* section.

APPLES BAKED IN WINE

4 baking apples, cored and 1-inch peel cut off top of each apple	½ cup apricot purée (See index for recipe)
1 cup red wine	2 tablespoons Cointreau

Place apples in baking dish and pour wine into dish. Bake in preheated 350° F. oven for 45 minutes, or until tender. Remove from oven and spoon wine from pan over apples. Let cool to room temperature. Combine Cointreau with apricot purée and spoon into apple centers.

Serves 4.

BLUEBERRY YOGURT DESSERT

2 pints plain yogurt
2 tablespoons honey
½ teaspoon vanilla
   extract
⅛ teaspoon powdered
   ginger

1 cup fresh blueberries,
   washed, drained, and
   stems removed

In bowl combine yogurt, honey, vanilla, and ginger. Fold in blueberries and chill thoroughly.

Serves 4.

BROILED GRAPEFRUIT

2 grapefruits, cut in
   half, seeded, and cut
   into sections with
   grapefruit knife

4 tablespoons honey

Spread each grapefruit half with honey and broil until top is golden.

Serves 4.

CANTALOUPE WITH FRUIT

2 cantaloupes, halved
   and seeded
1 pint strawberries,
   hulled, washed, and
   drained

2 cups blueberries,
   washed, drained, and
   stemmed
2 large ripe peaches,
   peeled, pitted, and
   sliced

Combine strawberries, blueberries, and peaches, and spoon into cantaloupe centers in equal amounts.

Serves 4.

FRESH FRUIT CUPS

1 ripe cantaloupe, halved, seeded, and cubed

1 ripe mango, peeled, pitted, and sliced

1 pint strawberries, washed, drained, and hulled

½ pint blueberries, washed and stemmed

2 fresh peaches, peeled, pitted, and sliced

4 ripe plums, peeled and sliced

½ pound seedless green grapes, stems removed

1 tablespoon lemon juice

2 tablespoons honey, or to taste

Combine ingredients in bowl. Cover and refrigerate for several hours.

Serves 6.

CHERRY COMPOTE

1 pound fresh Bing
    cherries, pitted
1 cup dry red wine

3 tablespoons sugar
1 cinnamon stick
1 slice fresh orange

In saucepan simmer cherries, wine and sugar with cinnamon stick and orange slice for 10 minutes. Remove cherries with slotted spoon to a bowl with cinnamon stick. Discard orange slice. Reduce liquid in saucepan over high heat for 5 minutes. Pour over cherries, cool, then chill for several hours.

Serves 4.

FRESH FIGS WITH RASPBERRIES

8 fresh ripe figs, peeled
    and quartered
1 pint fresh raspberries,
    washed and drained

8 tablespoons *crème
    fraîche* (See index
    for recipe)

Arrange 2 figs on individual serving plates and spoon equal amounts of raspberries in center. Spoon 2 tablespoons *crème fraîche* over each serving.

Serves 4.

FRESH FRUIT AND LEMON SHERBET

4 slices fresh pineapple
4 wedges cantaloupe
12 strawberries
8 slices fresh pear
small bunch green
grapes

12 grapefruit sections
4 plums
4 scoops lemon
sherbet (See index
for recipe)

Arrange fruit on individual dessert plates with small scoop of sherbet.

Serves 4.

FRESH FRUIT IN APRICOT YOGURT

1 Delicious apple,
peeled, cored, and
sliced
1 banana, sliced
1 fresh ripe pear,
peeled, cored, and
sliced
1 cup blueberries, stems
removed
½ cantaloupe, peeled,
seeds removed, and
cubed

1 cup plain yogurt
1 tablespoon sugar
6 ripe apricots, peeled,
pitted, and finely
chopped, or 8
unsweetened canned
apricots, finely
chopped

Place all fruit except apricots in bowl. Combine yogurt, sugar, and apricots. Add to fruit and gently toss.

Serves 4.

FRESH ORANGES IN SPICED WINE

4 navel oranges (peel
   and remove all white
   membrane, slice
   oranges)
¾ cup dry red wine

½ teaspoon powdered
   ginger
½ teaspoon cinnamon
2 whole cloves
1 tablespoon sugar

Combine all ingredients except orange slices in bowl.
Then add oranges, cover, and chill well.

Serves 4.

FRESH PEACH AND PLUM COMPOTE

4 firm but ripe peaches
4 firm but ripe plums
1 cup water
½ cup dry white wine

3 tablespoons sugar
1 vanilla bean
1 tablespoon peach
   brandy

Bring water and wine to a boil. Add peaches and
plums, and simmer for about 8 minutes. Remove fruit
and cool. Meanwhile add sugar and vanilla bean. Simmer
for 5 minutes. Remove skins from fruit and cut in
half. Remove seeds. Discard vanilla bean, pour ½ cup
of liquid over fruit in bowl, and add peach brandy.
Combine gently, cover, and refrigerate for several hours.

Serves 4.

FRESH PINEAPPLE WITH MANDARIN ORANGES AND CAMPARI

1 large ripe pineapple
1 8-ounce can mandarin
oranges, drained
¼ cup Campari

Cut pineapple into quarters lengthwise through green top. With sharp knife cut away core from each quarter. Then carefully release pulp from outer skin. Leave pulp in pineapple boat and slice crosswise in bite-sized pieces. Sprinkle 1 tablespoon Campari over each pineapple boat. Place mandarin oranges on toothpicks and stick into every other piece of pineapple.

Serves 4.

FRESH STRAWBERRIES WITH *CRÈME FRAÎCHE*

1 pint strawberries, washed, drained, and hulled
⅔ cup *crème fraîche* (See index for recipe)

Divide strawberries into 4 dessert bowls. Top with equal amounts of *crème fraîche*.

Serves 4.

GRILLED PINEAPPLE

8 slices fresh pineapple   2 tablespoons rum
4 tablespoons honey   1 teaspoon melted butter

Mix honey with rum and butter. Brush on both sides of pineapple slices and place on baking sheet lined with aluminum foil. Broil 3 inches from heat for 3 minutes. Turn and heat until golden.

Serves 4.

HONEYDEW MELON AND RASPBERRIES

1 honeydew melon   4 wedges of fresh lime
1 pint raspberries

Slice honeydew melon into quarters. Remove seeds. Fill centers with equal amounts of raspberries, and serve each with wedge of lime.

Serves 4.

LEMON SHERBET

2 cups skim milk
1 envelope plain gelatin
¾ cup sugar
⅓ cup fresh lemon juice

½ teaspoon vanilla extract
3 egg whites
salt

Soften gelatin in ¼ cup cold skim milk in bowl. Add remaining skim milk, sugar, lemon juice, and vanilla to saucepan and heat. Stir in gelatin mixture, and stir until gelatin has completely dissolved. Pour mixture into freezer tray and freeze until almost set. Place frozen mixture in large bowl. Add egg whites and dash of salt. Mix with electric beater until mixture is light and fluffy. Freeze until firm.

Serve in small portions.

Makes about 1 quart.

PEARS *MINCEUR*

2½ cups water
¼ cup sugar
2 tablespoons lemon
    juice

1 vanilla bean
6 pears, peeled, cored,
    and halved
fresh strawberries

Bring water to a boil with sugar, lemon juice, and vanilla bean, reduce heat, and simmer for 5 minutes. Add pears, cover, and simmer over low heat for 20 minutes. Cool, then chill thoroughly.

Garnish with fresh strawberries.

Serves 6.

PINEAPPLE AND STRAWBERRY ICE

1 cup pineapple purée
    and liquid
¼ cup sugar
⅔ cup water

1 envelope plain gelatin
½ cup puréed
    strawberries

Purée enough fresh pineapple to make 1 cup of pulp with liquid. Add sugar. Dissolve gelatin in 2 tablespoons water. Bring ⅔ cup water to a boil. Remove from heat and stir in gelatin until dissolved. Add to pineapple with puréed strawberries and combine well. Pour into individual dessert ramekins and freeze.

Garnish each with piece of fresh pineapple and a strawberry.

Serves 4.

ORANGE LEMON SNOW

1 envelope plain gelatin	¼ cup of sugar
¼ cup cold water	3 egg whites
¼ cup lemon juice	pinch of salt
1 cup orange juice	

Soften gelatin in cold water. Stir in lemon juice and sugar. Heat orange juice, add gelatin mixture, and stir until gelatin has dissolved. Chill for 30 minutes, or until mixture is just starting to thicken. Whip egg whites until stiff and fold into mixture. Pour into individual serving dishes and chill until set.

Serves 4.

SLICED ORANGES WITH STRAWBERRY SAUCE

4 large navel oranges, chilled	1 tablespoon sugar, or to taste
1 pint fresh strawberries	2 tablespoons kirsch

Peel rinds, including white pulp, off oranges. Slice each peeled orange into 6 even slices and arrange on individual dessert dishes. Place strawberries, sugar, and kirsch in food processor or blender, and purée. Spoon sauce, in equal portions, over oranges.

Serves 4.

STRAWBERRY SORBET SOUFFLÉ

1 envelope plain gelatin
⅓ cup water
2 teaspoons lemon juice
1 pint fresh strawberries,
    stems removed
1 tablespoon kirsch
3 tablespoons sugar
3 egg whites

Heat water and lemon juice to a boil and pour into blender. Add gelatin and blend. Add strawberries, sugar, and kirsch. Purée until smooth. Whip egg whites until smooth, and fold into strawberry mixture. Turn into soufflé dish and refrigerate until set.

Garnish with fresh strawberries.

Serves 4.

YOGURT DESSERT

1 cup plain yogurt
1 tablespoon sugar
    fruit, sliced or
    sectioned

Combine yogurt and sugar with any fruit such as a peach, banana, or pear and make a satisfying dessert. Of course, a mixture of fruit may be added, too.

About the Author

Michele Evans was born in Kansas and spent some formative "food-rich" summers on her grandparents' farm in Texas where she learned the fundamentals of cooking. There, she says, "Everything we ate was either grown or raised on the farm." A student of food throughout her life, she has studied at The London Cordon Bleu School of Cookery and at Le Cordon Bleu in Paris. She has also studied with James Beard, Simone Beck and Jacques Pépin. In 1976 Miss Evans was chosen to teach at the *New York Times Cooking School*.

Miss Evans frequently lectures on food and gives cooking demonstrations, where she emphasizes her belief in buying the freshest food you can find, preparing it simply, and serving it well. She is a frequent guest on *Good Morning America*.

Through her travels in Europe and the Caribbean, Miss Evans has built an extensive collection of international recipes. She believes that cookbook writers should make recipes as easy and clear as possible for cooks of all levels, an attitude that has made her cookbooks steady sellers for several years.

Miss Evans's other interests include travel, which she fits in between and in preparation for her books, photography, theater, and reading. The last two interests developed from her brief career as an actress (she has appeared in Mel Brooks's film, *The Producers*, and on Broadway with Alfred Drake in *Those That Play the Clowns*) and her work as a literary agent, until writing became a full-time occupation in 1975.

Michele has written six other cookbooks, all of which are still in print. Among them are *The Slow Crock Cookbook*, which is very popular, and *Fearless Cooking for Men*, a large basic cookbook, which will be published in the fall in hardcover.

Index

215

216

218

219

220

MORE GREAT COOKBOOKS FROM
WARNER BOOKS

THE BEST OF BESTSELLERS
FROM WARNER BOOKS!